Cambridge Elements ≡

The Philosophy of Immanuel Kant
edited by
Desmond Hogan
Princeton University

Howard Williams
University of Cardiff

Allen Wood
Indiana University, Bloomington

THE SUBLIME

Melissa M. Merritt
University of New South Wales

CAMBRIDGE
UNIVERSITY PRESS

CAMBRIDGE
UNIVERSITY PRESS

University Printing House, Cambridge CB2 8BS, United Kingdom

One Liberty Plaza, 20th Floor, New York, NY 10006, USA

477 Williamstown Road, Port Melbourne, VIC 3207, Australia

314–321, 3rd Floor, Plot 3, Splendor Forum, Jasola District Centre,
New Delhi – 110025, India

79 Anson Road, #06-04/06, Singapore 079906

Cambridge University Press is part of the University of Cambridge.

It furthers the University's mission by disseminating knowledge in the pursuit of
education, learning, and research at the highest international levels of excellence.

www.cambridge.org
Information on this title: www.cambridge.org/9781108438704
DOI: 10.1017/9781108529709

First published 2018

A catalogue record for this publication is available from the British Library.

ISBN 978-1-108-43870-4 Paperback
ISSN 2397-9461 (online)
ISSN 2514-3824 (print)

The Sublime

Melissa M. Merritt

Abstract: *The Element considers Kant's account of the sublime in the context of his predecessors in both the Anglophone and the German rationalist traditions. Since Kant says with evident endorsement that 'we call sublime that which is absolutely great'* (Critique of the Power of Judgment, *5:248) and nothing in nature can in fact be absolutely great (it can only figure as such, in certain presentations), Kant concludes that strictly speaking what is sublime can only be the human calling (*Bestimmung*) to perfect our rational capacity according to the standard of virtue that is thought through the moral law. The Element takes account of the difference between respect and admiration as the two main varieties of sublime feeling, and concludes by considering the role of Stoicism in Kant's account of the sublime, particularly through the channel of Seneca.*

Keywords: *sublime, Kant's aesthetics, aesthetic judgement, respect, Kantian moral psychology, Moses Mendelssohn, Seneca*

ISSNs: 2397-9461 (online), 2514-3824 (print)
ISBNs: 9781108438704 (PB), 9781108529709 (OC)

I took a walk the other morning, which I believe you would have admitted to be in the true sublime. I rambled till I got to the top of a hill, from whence I surveyed a vast extent of variegated country all round me, and the immense ocean beneath. I enjoyed this magnificent spectacle in all the freedom of absolute solitude. Not a house, or a human creature was within my view, nor a sound to be heard but the voice of the elements, the whistling winds, and rolling tide. I found myself deeply awed, and struck by this situation. The first impression it gave me was a sense of my own littleness, and I seemed shrinking to nothing in the midst of the stupendous objects by which I was surrounded. But I soon grew more important by the recollection that nothing which my eyes could survey, was of equal dignity with the human mind, at once the theatre and spectator of the wonders of Omnipotence. How vast are the capacities of the soul, and how little and contemptible its aims and pursuits? ... The view of great and astonishing objects is sometimes very useful, and gives a noble extension to the powers of the mind; but for wise ends, it is not formed to dwell long upon them, without a weariness that brings it back to its duties in the ordinary affairs of the world, and to common business and amusement. And so after all the elevation of the thoughts from a view of the sublime and stupendous objects of nature, one is very glad to return to enjoyments of a gentler kind, the song of linnets, and the bloom of roses.

Elizabeth Carter (poet, classicist, translator of Epictetus, and
Bluestocking) to Elizabeth Montagu, 2 July 1762

1 Prologue

So much was written about the sublime from the turn of the eighteenth century to Kant's 1790 *Critique of the Power of Judgment*, that it can seem as if every self-respecting philosopher and literary intellectual felt compelled to weigh in at some point, with at least passing remarks on the subject – though not very often with great technical precision, or searching consideration of the wider philosophical and systematic implications of the concept. Writers resorted to what starts to seem like a stock set of examples, drawing as much from travelogues and literary tradition as from personal experience – invoking, with considerable regularity, the sublimity of raging seas, expansive deserts, the Alps, the starry night sky, Genesis 1.3, the heroes of Homer, the Pyramids at Giza, and St Peter's in Rome. As a result, it is difficult to assess the originality of any early modern author on the sublime; and the sheer volume of writing on the topic defies efforts to trace historical narratives that develop in even increments, along straight and clearly marked paths.

How original is Kant's account of the sublime in the end? If we read widely enough, we seem to encounter many bits and pieces of it *avant la lettre*. And in some sense we do – except that Kant was a consummately systematic thinker, and whatever he borrows from tradition inevitably comes to mean something new as it takes its place in his own project. Moreover, the concept of the sublime is broadly germane to the problem that occupied Kant throughout his 'Critical' period and beyond: the epistemic and moral condition of human finitude. Although this problem has everything to do with the 'peculiar fate' of human reason that frames the opening remarks of the 1781 *Critique of Pure Reason* (Avii), the role of the sublime in Kant's effort to speak to this fate only begins to emerge with points of confluence between ethics and aesthetics in his later writings, from the 1788 *Critique of Practical Reason* onwards.[1]

Ultimately, for Kant, sublimity is the appreciation of absolute greatness from the human standpoint; and since by his lights the only determinate grasp we can have of such greatness is *practical*, the Kantian sublime has an irrevocably moral source. I make that case in the middle sections of this Element; the framing sections focus (albeit selectively, owing to constraints on space) on the historical context of Kant's work on the sublime. Although others have recognised the need to consider Kant's aesthetics in historical context, most exclusively consider his relation to the Anglophone tradition; fewer consider the significance of German aesthetic rationalism, and especially Moses Mendelssohn, for the development of Kant's theory of the sublime (but consider, more recently, Guyer 2014, Brady 2013, Rayman 2012). I begin by sketching the contours of

---

[1] There is little discussion in the following of Kant's pre-critical (1764) *Observations on the Feeling of the Beautiful and Sublime* (found in Kant 2007: 23–62), a work that lies largely outside of the orbit of Kant's concerns in the critical period; but Kant does there extol, albeit in passing, the sublimity of apathy, and virtue (2:215–6) – topics that concern me below.

Kant's theory in relation to some of the key moves of these earlier modern traditions.

As will become clear, I take the topic of the sublime to be closely linked to Kant's ethics and moral psychology. I am by no means alone in recognising this connection, or in emphasising it. So the interpretation is not, simply as such, controversial. However, some prominent commentators (e.g. Budd 2008, 2002) take this link to be a failing in Kant's account of the sublime. The natural response to this perceived failure is either to abandon Kant, or to recast a Kantian theory of the sublime in a purely aesthetic sphere, divorcing it from its original relation to ethics and moral psychology.[2] I do not go down this route because the textual evidence for the moral underpinnings of the Kantian sublime is so strong. One of my broader aims is to improve our understanding of this evidence, and the connection between morality and sublimity more generally. As I have studied these matters in recent years, I have been struck by the relative absence of scholarly attention to the Stoic influences on Kant's moral psychology and, by extension, on his theory of the sublime.[3] Thus, another general aim is to expand the historical contextualisation of Kant's theory of the sublime beyond its relation to early modern sources. My concluding remarks open up that line of inquiry, with particular attention to the role of Seneca.

---

[2] Forsey (2007) recognises that such a move calls for leaving Kant behind, which she is prepared to do; more strikingly, she argues that any coherent theory of the sublime requires Kantian systematic commitments (the rejection of which calls for taking the sublime to be untheorisable). Other efforts to develop a more 'aesthetic' interpretation of the Kantians sublime proceed through the reconstruction of his views about the sublimity in art, e.g. in Doran (2015) and Crowther (1989).

[3] The topic has been developed more in relation to moral psychology, beginning with Sherman (1997); regarding the sublime in particular, note the passing remark of Allison (2001:344). Santozki (2012) offers helpful scholarship on Kant's relation to Stoicism and German neo-Stoicism, and notes some rhetorical similarities between Kant and Seneca on the sublimity of the starry heavens.

For helpful comments on earlier drafts, I wish to thank Allen Wood and an anonymous reviewer for Cambridge University Press. Research for this piece was supported by a grant from the Australian Research Council (DP130100172).

2 The Kantian Sublime: A Conceptual and Historical Map

'We call **sublime** that which is **absolutely great**' (CJ 5:248): so begins Kant's dedicated account of the sublime in the *Critique of the Power of Judgment*.[4] Beginning thus, Kant points to a broader tradition of thought about the sublime: the 'we' who take sublimity to consist in absolute greatness. My aim in this section is to unpack this remark to reveal the larger conceptual contours of Kant's own conception of the sublime, and the historical context in which it developed.

2.1 Kant's Starting Point

Let us begin, as Kant himself does, by noting that the idea of greatness is indeterminate: we speak of greatness in many ways. We speak of great political powers, great winds, and great heights; of great beauty and great character. Kant is interested in the idea of greatness with all the flexibility of the Latin *magnitudo* – which, in its literal meaning, is greatness of size or number, but in its figurative meanings can pertain to greatness of soul, greatness of rank or dignity, and so on.[5]

Kant, however, begins with greatness considered in its most literal sense, as magnitude of size or bulk. Can anything be absolutely great in size? Kant invokes 'absolute' in the strict sense, so that what is at issue is a magnitude *not comparable* to any other (CJ 5:248).[6] Even the immensity of the Milky Way is comparable to, because measurable in terms of, so many widths of the Earth (5:256). And since, for Kant, nature is not a mere order of inert extended things, but

---

[4] In shorthand: the third *Critique* (CJ). The first two sections of the third *Critique's* Analytic of the Sublime (CJ §§23–4) concern the *division* between the appreciation of beauty and sublimity as two modes of the 'aesthetic judgment of reflection'. This mode of judgement is the overarching concern of Part I of CJ, the Critique of the Aesthetic Power of Judgment. The quoted remark is the 'nominal definition of the sublime' at the outset of CJ §25.

[5] Charlton and Short s.v. *magnitudo* (1879:1099). Kant has here distinguished 'being great' and 'being a quantity' (*groß sein* and *eine Größe sein*), with the respective Latin glosses *magnitudo* and *quantitas*.

[6] Kant glosses his own German phrase *schlechthin groß* with the Latin *absolute, non comparative magnum* (5:248).

a system of forces,[7] it should follow as well that there can be no absolute greatness of power in nature. There are, of course, many forces of nature that 'we gladly call' sublime: 'thunder clouds towering up into the heavens, bringing with them flashes of lightning and crashes of thunder, volcanoes with their all-destroying violence, hurricanes with the devastation they leave behind, the boundless ocean set into a rage, a lofty waterfall on a mighty river' (5:261). But even the greatest destructive force we can think of – say, the Tsar Bomba – has a power that is comparable to, because measurable in terms of, that of some number of horses. Nature, the order of phenomena, consists of relations – and whatever immensity we can encounter in nature can only ever be relatively great.

So we should not be surprised by Kant's repeated insistence that stormy seas and the like are not, strictly speaking, *sublime*: 'sublimity is not contained in nature, but only in our mind' (CJ 5:264; see also 5: 245–6, 250, 256, 280). But surely the human mind *has* a place in nature, and can accordingly be influenced, and shaped, by nature. So Kant's move – namely, saying that true sublimity can only lie in our mind – does not by itself make room for a conception of sublimity as absolute greatness. Other philosophical commitments are required. If true sublimity is absolute greatness, and therefore cannot be found in nature, then the absolute greatness at issue must lie in some kind of freedom from the causal order of material nature – a freedom that expresses itself in the self-determination of a rational being. For imperfectly rational beings – for *us* – such self-determination is won, if at all, through struggle and effort. In full flower, this self-determination is virtue. As a result, the sublime is not an exclusively 'aesthetic' topic for Kant. The Analytic of the Sublime in the *Critique of the Power of Judgment* is not a closed system: it points outside of itself, to a larger set of concerns about the nature of human reason, and its cultivation in the face of our finitude or embodiment. The central sections of this Element (§§3–4) will

---

[7] See MFNS, especially chapter 2 (on Dynamics). This point bears on Kant's division between 'mathematical' and 'dynamical' modes of the sublime, which I consider in §3.

make a case for that overarching thesis – that by Kant's lights *what is sublime*, strictly speaking, is our disposition to virtue.

Here, though, I want to shed light on the historical background against which he arrives at this view. For quite a lot was written about the sublimity of stormy seas and high peaks before Kant; and so we should be struck that he begins with the idea that 'we' take sublimity to consist in absolute greatness, and then proceeds to make such quick work of the idea that anything like a stormy sea is actually sublime. Who is this 'we'? It turns out that the answer to this question is not entirely straightforward, for relatively few of Kant's predecessors explicitly conceived of sublimity in terms of absolute greatness.[8] We will thus need to take stock of some of what had been written about the sublime in the decades prior to Kant's Analytic of the Sublime to understand why it might be justifiable for Kant to begin in this way.

2.2 The Anglophone Tradition and the Reflective Turn

It is widely held that eighteenth-century Anglophone work on the sublime is distinguished by its emphasis on the 'direct' experience of sublimity of nature, and that this marks a departure from the ancient Hellenistic text that in some sense set the initial agenda for modern discussions of the sublime, Longinus's *On the Sublime* (*Peri Hypsous*).[9] For Longinus's treatise – or the part of it that has survived – is basically a work of poetics, broadly construed: it focuses on how different styles and forms of writing can produce

---

[8] Thus, Budd's (2008:16) remark that Kant's conception of the sublime as absolute greatness is 'idiosyncratic' may seem fair enough. But it is historically insensitive: the idea figures explicitly in the German rationalist tradition, and implicitly in a neglected line of thought in the Anglophone tradition (as we will see in §2.3–4).

[9] The authorship of *Peri Hypsous* is contested; but for the sake of convenience I will refer to this author as 'Longinus' – a Hellenistic author, likely of the first century AD. Longinus greatly impacted the development of modern aesthetics, first through Boileau's 1674 French translation, and then through John Dennis's discussion of Longinus in his 1701 *Advancement and Reformation of Poetry* and 1704 *Grounds of Criticism in Poetry*. He is mentioned passim throughout the ensuing Anglophone tradition. We will return, briefly, to Longinus in §5.2.

sublimity, which he implicitly takes to be a specially elevated state of mind.[10] I take the core thesis about eighteenth-century Anglophone tradition on the sublime to be broadly correct, though I suspect it has been somewhat overstated by its proponents.[11] For the Anglophone writers *did* direct fresh and sustained attention to the direct experience of nature as a source of a particular elevation of mind deemed 'sublime'.

We thus hear quite a bit from them about the sublimity of vast, open vistas – and particularly of what is raw, inhospitable, and uncultivated: hostile stretches of desert; deep and dark forests; swelling seas with titanic, crashing waves; sharp, overhanging cliffs; craggy, icy, peaks piled high atop one another – all are said, time and again, to be *sublime*.[12] But while Anglophone writers took particular interest in nature's 'rude kind of magnificence' (to invoke Joseph Addison's wonderful phrase[13]), they also drew attention to the sublimity of works of human ingenuity and architecture: Stonehenge, the Egyptian pyramids, St Peter's in Rome,

---

[10] The expressions for 'the sublime' in Greek, Latin, and German are substantival forms of verbs meaning 'to raise or lift up' – ὑψόω, *sublīmo*, and *erheben* respectively – with English deriving from Latin. Thus, what is sublime is elevated, lofty, etc.

[11] Brady (2013) adopts the received view of the Anglophone tradition, taking it to prioritise sublimity of nature over sublimity of art, ideas, and abstract objects (such as virtue) (for a telling passage, see 2013:35-6). But she risks overstatement at times – e.g., in her treatment of Addison as the key figure in this prioritisation of the sublimity of nature, while maintaining perfect silence about his earlier *Spectator* essays on the sublimity of *Paradise Lost*. Here Budick (2010) can seem a welcome corrective, as he suggests that we distort Kant if we take him as adopting the (putative) Anglophone prioritisation of the sublimity of nature wholesale. But his positive thesis that Kant's account of the sublime was the product of an intense, sustained, and highly sophisticated literary engagement with Milton is implausible, owing to insufficient evidence that Kant had the requisite skill in English – a fact by which Budick is curiously unmoved (2010:53-4).

[12] See, e.g., Addison, *Spectator* nos. 412 and 417 (Bond 1965 [v.3]:540 and 564); Baillie, *Essay on the Sublime* (Ashfield and Bolla 1996:88); for Burke on the sublimity of forests, see *Enquiry* II.xxii and III.xvi (1990:78 and 105), on stormy oceans II.ii (53-4), and on craggy peaks II.vii (66).

[13] Addison, *Spectator* no. 412 (Bond 1965 [v.3]:540).

and the Great Wall of China figure just as well in the Anglophone theorist's stock set of examples.[14]

But none of these things, from the vastness of deserts to the stupendous Great Wall, obviously offers a presentation of *absolute greatness*. We should then wonder whether any idea of 'absolute greatness' enters into Anglophone writing on the sublime. The beginnings of an answer may lie in another distinguishing feature of the Anglophone tradition: they tended not to treat the sublimity of nature as an end in itself, but rather presented the greatness of nature as a certain stimulus by which the subject's attention might be thrust back onto herself. Commentators sometimes speak of this as a dawning 'subjectivism' about the sublime;[15] but this label is potentially misleading, inasmuch as it might suggest something contingent or one-off, when most accounts take the enjoyment of natural sublimity to reveal something universal, and possibly necessary, about us as human beings. Hence, I will refer to this development in theories of the sublime as the *reflective turn*, i.e. the idea is that the appreciation of natural sublimity allows us to revel in something about our own minds that is ordinarily hidden.

If the reflective turn provides an interpretive frame for the Anglophone tradition, it is nevertheless one that gets filled in a wide range of ways – depending, above all, on what exactly the enjoyment of natural sublimity is supposed to reveal about us. But the reflective turn does not, by itself, underwrite a conception of sublimity as absolute greatness. It conceivably underwrites the thought that what is strictly speaking sublime may not lie in any immensity of nature, but rather in some quality of mind by which

---

[14] These were not always experienced firsthand: travelogues were an important source. Kames invokes the Great Pyramid and St Peter's in the same breath (2005:151) – as does Kant nearly three decades later (CJ 5:252), though citing Nicolas Savary's 1787 *Lettres sur l'Égypte* for the pyramids (see also Gerard [1759:23]). Addison, who did travel to Italy, also mentions the pyramids and the Great Wall: *Spectator* no. 415 (Bond 1965 [v.3]:555). On the sublimity of Stonehenge, see Burke, *Enquiry* II.xii (1990:71).

[15] E.g. Monk's thesis that the developing 'subjectivism' of the Anglophone tradition is eventually brought out in full flower by Kant (1960:4–6).

such immensity is enjoyed. But a further step would be needed: namely, that the revealed quality of mind is itself absolutely great. Thomas Reid may have come closest to this idea in the Anglophone tradition. For Reid, any sublimity or grandeur 'discerned in objects of sense' is itself a kind of reflection of a sublimity or grandeur in our own minds (somewhat as the moon reflects the light of the sun) – where this original sublimity is a quality of mind worthy of the highest, or most 'enthusiastical admiration', because it has 'real and intrinsic excellence'.[16] But without further elaboration, this still falls short of the idea that what is truly sublime is *absolutely great*.

Since, as we will see in §3, Kant does make use of the reflective turn in his account of natural sublimity, we should consider some of the range of ways in which it plays out in the Anglophone tradition. Its origin is plausibly traced to Joseph Addison's ground-breaking essays on the 'pleasures of the imagination' published in the *Spectator* in 1712. Early on, Addison observes that it is not so much 'the bulk of any single object' that we consider sublime, 'but the largeness of a whole view, considered as one entire piece'.[17] Sublimity is thus explained to be not so much a feature of objects, but rather a feature of how we take things in. This is the beginning of the reflective turn that was developed by subsequent theorists of the sublime. Although the reflective turn can be found throughout the Anglophone tradition, we will briefly consider just two examples that contrast on key points relevant to Kant's later development of the reflective turn: John Baillie's 1747 *Essay on the Sublime*, and Edmund Burke's 1757 *Philosophical Enquiry into the Origin of our Ideas of the Sublime and Beautiful*.[18]

---

[16] See Reid (1969:778 and 768).

[17] *Spectator* no. 412 (Bond 1965 [v.3]:540). Addison speaks of the 'grandeur' of nature in these essays – but it is an account of natural *sublimity* (in fact he reserves the term 'sublime' for poetry, in his essays on Milton).

[18] Kant quotes Burke in the Analytic of the Sublime (CJ 5:277; see also FI 20:238), from Christian Garve's 1773 German translation. However, Kant would not likely have known Baillie's work; and very little is now known about Baillie, except that he was a physician and his *Essay* was published posthumously (Monk 1960:72n26). Nevertheless, Baillie's *Essay* contains ideas that were later

In each case, it will be important to distinguish not only the particular version of the reflective turn, but also the attendant account of why the reflection should be *pleasing*. Addison's halting effort to consider why the sublime pleases only serves to bring the problem itself into sharper view. 'Our imagination loves to be filled with an object, or to grasp at anything that is too big for its capacity', he contends; 'We are flung into a pleasing astonishment at such unbounded views, and feel a delightful stillness and amazement in the soul at the apprehension of them'.[19] But why, really, should we be pleased by what is altogether too much for us to handle? Addison has no compelling answer, beyond the assertion that we enjoy the lack of constraint when we take in a vista that, we feel, could occupy us endlessly – 'a spacious horizon is an image of liberty' – and that God has made us so that we take this particular pleasure in the apprehension of whatever is, or at least seems, 'great or unlimited'.[20] But Ballie's and Burke's answers take a different form: both contend that the sublimity of nature *exercises* the mind in ways that are properly enjoyable – an idea that, in general outline at least, survives in Kant's later account.

2.2.1 Baillie

Baillie asserts a certain priority of the sublimity of nature over sublimity in poetry, arguing that the latter can only arise from the apt description of the former. He then claims that the apprehension of a 'grand object' exercises and 'expands' the mind 'to a kind of immensity', drawing first on the example of the starry night sky:

> Thus in viewing the heavens, how the soul is elevated; and stretching itself to larger scenes and more extended prospects, in a noble enthusiasm of grandeur quits the narrow earth, darts from planet to planet, and takes in worlds at one view! Hence comes the name of

developed by Gerard and Kames – whose works Kant certainly did know, as he mentions them in his notes and lectures (e.g. Refl 1588 [16:27], Refl 3160 [16:688], and JL 9:15 on Henry Home, Lord Kames and Refl 949 [15:420] on Gerard).

[19] *Spectator* no. 412 (Bond 1965 [v.3]: 540).

[20] *Spectator* no. 412 (Bond 1965 [v.3]: 541) and no. 413 (545).

the sublime to every thing which thus raises the mind to fits of
greatness ... hence arises that exultation and pride which the
mind ever feels from the consciousness of its own vastness – that
object can only be justly called the sublime, which in some degree
disposes the mind to this enlargement of itself, and gives her a lofty
conception of her own powers.   (Ashfield and de Bolla 1996:88)

Natural immensity 'stretches' the mind, and ultimately
'expands' it. What we *enjoy* seems to be not so much the physical
immensity that provides the stimulus for this exercise, but rather
the exercise itself – or, at least, how it makes available the mind's
own powers. Moreover, Baillie elaborates, sublimity requires more
than physical vastness. It also requires, first, an element of novelty
or surprise, since 'two or three days at sea would sink all that
elevated pleasure we feel upon viewing a vast ocean' (90);
and second, a certain uniformity so that one can take in an immensity in one go, without having to register and unify a range of
disparate elements. When 'the mind must run from object to
object', Baillie contends, it can 'never get a full and complete
prospect' (89).[21]

Why should this be pleasurable? Baillie answers that it is
pleasurable in much the same way that physical exercise is
pleasurable – at least when we don't find the exercise difficult.
Of course, exercise often *is* difficult, precisely because we have
little power to do it. But Baillie doesn't consider this: for him,
the enjoyment of the sublime is linked to the freshly discov-
ered ease of exercising certain mental powers. The powers
themselves (whatever they may be: he is not explicit) seem
not to stand in need of cultivation; rather, they lie in wait,
perfectly formed and ready to be stimulated by natural
immensity to an exercise that will bring these very powers

---

[21] For a similar account of the role of uniformity, see Gerard, *Essay on Taste* I.ii
(1759:15–16). Given that Baillie had just spoken of one's attention darting 'from
planet to planet', this is somewhat curious; but presumably his point is that the
night sky offers a certain uniformity of texture, even though there are no regular
patterns to the stars, and that this uniformity in turn allows for an apparently
comprehensive take on the greatness of the starry heavens.

into view, so that the mind may 'admire … her own perfection' (90).

Baillie thus contends that the enjoyment of sublimity must be rooted in some appreciation of our own positive powers, not in any lack of power or weakness. Later on (§§3.3.2, 4.1–2, and 4.4) we will see that Kant incorporates such a point into his account of the pleasures of the sublime, though Moses Mendelssohn was, in all likelihood, his proximate influence on this issue. Baillie also traces the pleasures in apprehending natural sublimity to the point just raised about how uniformity allows us to apprehend an immensity in one view – and thus, presumably, with some kind of *ease*. Though this idea was not unique to Baillie (we find it also in Kames's *Elements of Criticism*, a work Kant clearly knew[22]), it was not one that Kant accepted. For Kant, as we will see (§§3–4), the enjoyment of the sublime involves some kind of struggle or difficulty, as a precondition. Of Kant's Anglophone predecessors, Edmund Burke provides the starkest example of an account that emphasises both that we enjoy natural sublimity because it reveals something otherwise hidden about our own minds (the reflective turn), and that this experience of the sublime involves an element of pain or struggle.

2.2.2 Burke

Edmund Burke's 1757 treatise, *A Philosophical Enquiry into the Origin of our Ideas of the Sublime and Beautiful*, undoubtedly influenced Kant's account of the sublime in both positive and negative ways. Burke drew a much sharper division between beauty and sublimity than any of his predecessors had done, taking our appreciation of each to be rooted in distinct interests of human nature: our enjoyment of beauty is rooted in 'our' desire for 'society of the sexes', while our enjoyment of sublimity arouses the animating passions of self-preservation.[23] 'Whatever is fitted in any sort to

---

[22] Kames (2005:150–78; see esp. 161).

[23] See especially Burke (1990:35–8 and 47). In characterising the desire for 'society of the sexes', Burke assumes an inflection of this desire that is both

excite the ideas of pain, and danger, that is to say, whatever is in any sort terrible, or is conversant about terrible objects, or operates in a manner analogous to terror, is a source of the *sublime*; that is, it is productive of the strongest emotion the mind is capable of feeling' (1990:36). We appreciate the sublime through a feeling Burke calls 'delight', which he distinguishes from positive pleasure, as an agreeableness 'that accompanies the removal of pain or danger' (34). Hence, there must be some assault on our sense of safety to engage the passions associated with self-preservation; but if we are to revel in these passions, and *enjoy* them in some way, we must also recognise our real safety from danger.

Given Burke's view that the source of the sublime lies in the instinct of self-preservation, we should not be surprised to find that he emphasises the sublimity of power over the sublimity of size.[24] Burke analyses the sublime in terms of the various properties of sensible representations that are liable to arouse the feelings associated with the drive for self-preservation – for example, extreme (and disorienting) contrasts of light and dark. A common theme is the importance of obscurity: any experience of the sublime must somehow tap into feelings of terror, and such feelings are heightened when we lack a clear view of 'the full extent of any danger' (54). The enjoyment of the sublime will thus begin with a horrifying prospect that offers a kind of shock to the mind – 'all its motions are suspended, with some degree of horror' – followed by a delight that registers, paradigmatically, in the feeling of astonishment (53). Or consider Burke on the appearance of infinity, which he claims relies upon the repetition of uniform sensation – successive gushes of waterfall, or crosses in a military cemetery: you find no bounds of

heterosexual and male; however, his account of beauty is thankfully not my topic here.

[24] As a result, Burke can claim sublimity for small poisonous beasts – but takes feelings of sublimity to be enhanced when greatness of power and size are conjoined: a vista of an extended level plain 'is certainly no mean idea', he observes, but a stormy seascape is all the more affecting because it is 'an object of no small terror', combining greatness of extent with greatness of power (1990:53–4).

the thing, 'the same object still seems to continue, and the imagination has no rest' (1990:67–8). With all this, Burke contends that we enjoy the sublime through some kind of assault on our cognitive powers, so that they either seize up or else are rendered exhausted. But why, again, should this be pleasing?

Burke offers two different, and largely unconnected, answers to this question. First, he takes the basic principle of our enjoyment of sublimity to be that it engages our instinct for self-preservation, and arouses its attendant passions. The apprehension of something assaulting can be enjoyable if we appreciate our own real safety, for this allows us to savour our strongest passions, rather than simply be actuated by them.[25] Thus, we experience something like an overcoming of danger, which is grounds for *delight* in Burke's terms. But Burke's second account, offered considerably later in the *Enquiry*, is closer in outline to Baillie's: natural sublimity arouses the mind to a kind of exercise. The 'finer and more delicate organs' of the mind need exercise as much as the 'coarser organs' of muscle and limb (1990:122), and our enjoyment of the sublime is ultimately the enjoyment of this exercise. This, too, involves overcoming difficulty: for whereas Baillie assumes that the capacity to apprehend immensity is ready and waiting, and we are *pleased* to do it so *easily*, Burke contends that natural sublimity arouses our capacities to a difficult labour, or struggle. And while Baillie assumes that a complete apprehension of the immensity is possible owing to its 'uniformity', Burke supposes that we enjoy the sublime only when we are confronted with an immensity that we can never completely take in.[26] Since these are the struggles we must endure to keep ourselves in a state of health, Burke contends that our enjoyment of the sublime may be

---

[25] See Burke (1990:47 and 121–2). See also Addison, *Spectator* no. 418, on why the feelings of terror and pity that can be aroused through sublime poetry can be enjoyed: we enjoy not so much the 'description of what is terrible' but 'the reflection we make on ourselves at the time of reading it', so that the pleasure lies in the solace of our recognised safety (Bond 1965 [v.3]:568).

[26] Kant's later view of mathematical sublimity draws from Burke on this point (see §3.3.1).

analysed as the delight we take in the 'surmounting of [such] difficulties' (1990:122–3).

As we will see in §3, Kant's account of why natural sublimity pleases shares certain features of what we have seen exemplified in the Anglophone tradition – and perhaps particularly in Burke. For Kant, natural sublimity assaults and moves the mind in ways that challenge it, and arouses feelings akin to the moral feeling of respect. But by Kant's lights we enjoy natural sublimity inasmuch as we take an interest in our own moral cultivation.[27] In some sense, this is closer to Burke than to Baillie, owing to the difficulty that is involved in cultivating these powers. But while Kant adopts the idea that natural sublimity occasions a kind of exercise that supports a certain kind of health, for him this can only be a *moral* health, a proper expression of the human being as an essentially *rational* animal.

2.3 Early German Rationalism on the Sublime

To find sublimity explicitly conceived as absolute greatness, we need to turn to the German tradition of aesthetic rationalism that developed from Alexander Baumgarten's 1750 *Aesthetica*.[28]

German aesthetic rationalism is rooted in the distinction between sensible and intellectual cognition developed by Leibniz and Wolff: sensible cognition grasps in a 'confused' manner what can only be grasped 'distinctly' through the intellect's explicit, and principle-based, articulation of the parts of a thing and determination of its place in a systematic whole. But while the rationalists take sensible cognition to be *confused* in its very nature, they recognise that it can nevertheless be *clear* – vividly present to mind – and may even possess a perfection proper to its nature. Baumgarten introduces aesthetics as a practical 'science of sensible cognition' (*Aesthetica* §1 [2007:10–11]) that has the 'perfection

---

[27] In §3, we will assess how this point accords with other aspects of his theory, such as 'disinterestedness' of aesthetic judgements of reflection.

[28] *Aesthetica* was published in two volumes, in 1750 and 1758 respectively, and was never completed.

of sensible cognition' as its 'purpose' – where this perfection is nothing other than *beauty* (*Aesthetica* §14 [2007:20–1]). He lists six aspects of beauty, the second of which is the 'aesthetic magnitude' of the cognition – or, effectively, its *sublimity* (*Aesthetica* §22 [2007:24–5]).[29] Hence, sublimity is an aspect of beauty for Baumgarten and his followers, rather than essentially distinct from it.

But what is 'aesthetic magnitude'? Georg Meier, Baumgarten's student and self-professed expositor, explains this magnitude as the greatness of what is represented: a cognition with aesthetic magnitude represents 'great, suitable, important, noble objects', and does so in a manner suitable to such dignified content.[30] Although this arguably sums up Baumgarten's conclusions on the topic, Baumgarten himself begins with the more literal notion of magnitude as greatness in size. He also draws some other distinctions in the neighbourhood, and is not explicit about whether or how they align: aesthetic magnitude may be either 'relative' or 'absolute', and it can be 'natural' or 'moral' (*Aesthetica* §178 and §181 [2007:154–5,156–7]). Relative magnitude is comparative, whereas absolute magnitude is unconditional and complete in itself, so that nothing further can be added to it (*Aesthetica* §179 and §185 [2007:154–5,160–1]). Natural and moral magnitude, on the other hand, are distinguished in terms of their relation to freedom: natural magnitude *is not*, whereas moral magnitude *is*, closely connected to the idea of freedom as it is determined 'in accordance with moral laws' (*Aesthetica* §§181–2 [2007:156–9]).

Where British writers so often found sublimity in the high seas, Baumgarten takes forests as paradigmatic of the mighty deep: 'Forests possess the greatest relative magnitude. They are worthy

---

[29] Baumgarten analyses beauty in terms of the 'wealth, magnitude, truth, clarity, certitude, and liveliness' of the cognition (*Aesthetica* §22 [2007:24–5]), and proceeds to take these aspects in turn. Aesthetic magnitude, where sublimity falls, is addressed in *Aesthetica* §§177–216.

[30] Meier (1757:46–7); see Guyer (2014:330) for a translation of the relevant passage (*Betrachtungen* §22). Beiser (2009:123) notes scholarly controversy over whether Meier accurately presents the letter and spirit of Baumgarten.

of the greatest honour and are in an eminent way GREAT, MEANINGFUL, AND SUBLIME' (*Aesthetica* §203 [2007:176–7]). Yet as he remarks on their prodigious, yet relative, greatness, he pauses to quote a passage from the Roman Stoic moral philosopher, Seneca. The interlude is curious: for just as Baumgarten says that forests are sublime, he thereupon remarks that he 'would not quarrel' with Seneca, who says that 'Only virtue is sublime and exalted [*sublimis et excelsa*]' (*De Ira* I.21.4 [Seneca 2010:34]). How can he say in his own voice that forests are sublime, at the same time as he endorses Seneca's view that only virtue is sublime?[31] Perhaps he means to suggest that the attested sublimity of forests (and the like) must somehow be ultimately rooted in, and dependent upon, the sublimity of virtue – after all, he does not say that natural magnitude is unconnected with the concept of freedom, but rather that it is less closely connected to it than moral magnitude is. But if this is his view, it remains implicit at best. Fortunately we can turn to Seneca's text for some guidance.

Seneca had been arguing against a common view of the greatness of anger: namely, that a person enraged can go on to do 'great' things – astonishing things that he wouldn't ordinarily have the drive to do (*De Ira* I.20–1). He then observes that lust and ambition also impel people in such ways, and that there is, more obviously, nothing great about them. Baumgarten's quotation picks up Seneca's point that 'all vices' (anger and other such faults) may be 'great' in the sense that their influence over human behaviour can be far-reaching and profound, but they are not great in the sense of being valuable, or worthy of choice. Perhaps anger has a kind of relative magnitude, as it impels us in ways that can in principle be overpowered. But whatever has absolute magnitude, on Baumgarten's own account, must be unconditional and

---

[31] Baumgarten says that he would question only Seneca's next sentence, that the greatness of virtue requires tranquillity, through freedom from emotion (i.e., Stoic apathy). Although Baumgarten and others in the German rationalist tradition were influenced by Stoicism, they do not tend to endorse the Stoic ideal of apathy; I will return to this point, vis-à-vis Kant's relation to Mendelssohn on the sublime, in §5.

complete within itself – lacking in nothing. And this is how the Stoic conceives of virtue.[32] Thus, by endorsing this part of Seneca's conclusion, Baumgarten implies that sublimity as *absolute* greatness must ultimately be a matter of moral perfection.

Our aim here is not to resolve the tensions and clarify the ambiguities of Baumgarten's account of the sublime. For present purposes, it is enough to recognise that he draws a distinction between natural and moral magnitude, and that this distinction correlates to some extent with the distinction between relative and absolute magnitude. Presumably any natural magnitude must also be relative. Perhaps not all moral magnitudes are absolute: this might follow if there are other moral magnitudes apart from virtue, or if it is supposed that virtue admits of degree. Here we would do well to remember that Baumgarten's entire discussion falls under the scope of *aesthetic* magnitude – so whatever he may be conceiving as moral magnitude in this context can only be what admits of sensible presentation:[33] e.g., virtue as it may be suggested in the poetic and plastic arts, or as it may make itself manifest, however uncertainly, in normal human observation of action and character.

2.4 Taking Stock

We have been looking briefly and selectively into Kant's predecessors in order to understand how he could set out with the claim that 'we call **sublime** that which is **absolutely great**' (CJ 5:248).[34] We do not find a widespread invocation of sublimity as absolute greatness in the Anglophone tradition; instead, we characteristically find particular attention to natural immensity, which can only

---

[32] This is a fundamental tenet of Stoic ethics, rooted in the view that virtue alone is truly good; from Seneca, see e.g. *Letters* 76.6–16 (2015:240–1).

[33] See *Aesthetica* §211 (2007:184–5).

[34] Although this 'nominal definition' of the sublime comes at the start of Kant's account of *mathematical* sublimity (CJ §25), and thus might be assumed to concern only what figures as absolutely great *in size*, I will argue in §3 that it governs Kant's account of our enjoyment of natural sublimity broadly – including the *dynamical* sublime (i.e., that which figures as absolutely great *in power*).

be comparative. To find an idea of sublimity as absolute greatness, we need to turn to the German rationalist tradition – where the possibility of such sublimity is rooted in the moral perfection of virtue. It would be rash to conclude, from this, that Kant takes himself to be having a conversation with his German rationalist predecessors alone. For what Kant is evidently setting out to do is combine the Anglophone tradition's reflective turn with the German rationalists' readiness to link true sublimity – or absolute greatness – with the moral perfection of virtue.

Thus, Kant takes our enjoyment of natural sublimity to be reflective along the same general lines set out by the Anglophone tradition, but takes the revealed power, or propensity, of mind to be absolutely great. His invocation of the reflective turn is plain enough, as he says time and again that 'true sublimity must be sought only in the mind of the one who judges' and not in the natural object that is better conceived as a mere occasioning stimulus (CJ 5:256). *What is* sublime is something about our own minds, specifically some capacity for self-determination independently of nature. Thus, Kant aims to argue that

> sublimity is not contained in anything in nature, but only in our mind, insofar as we can become conscious of being superior [*überlegen*] to nature within us and thus also to nature outside us (insofar as it influences us).   (CJ 5:264)

Kant says here that something about the mind is 'superior' to nature – where this superiority is cashed out as the possibility of its independence from nature's influence or determination. In §3 we will see how and why this should amount to an idea of sublimity as absolute greatness by Kant's lights.

We will be better positioned to undertake that work if we consider, by way of conclusion, another line of thought in the Anglophone tradition – one that moves from the bare consideration of natural immensity to this as the work of God. For it is here that a conception of sublimity as absolute greatness makes a halting, and largely implicit, appearance in the Anglophone tradition. We can find it already in Addison, in a later contribution to the *Spectator* that he passed off as another's reply to his earlier essays on the 'pleasures of the imagination':

> A troubled ocean, to a man who sails upon it, is, I think, the biggest object that he can see in motion, and consequently gives his mind one of the highest kinds of pleasure that can arise from greatness. I must confess, it is impossible for me to survey this world of fluid matter, without thinking on the hand that first poured it out, and made a proper channel for its reception.[35]

Reid makes much the same point more than seventy years later – that the sea and the starry heavens and so forth are vast objects that require 'a stretch of imagination to grasp them in our minds. But they appear truly grand, and merit the highest admiration, when we consider them as the work of God'.[36] Such remarks figure as outliers in a view of the Anglophone tradition as characterised by the reflective turn, since what we admire is not our own minds but the divine power of creation.[37]

However, it is worth pointing out that the sea and the starry night sky are linked to quite different conceptions of natural sublimity. The sea is a blank expanse, and, if it is raging, then sheer power. It is vast but not articulated, not complex. It is particularly important to the Anglophone writers. The starry night sky is an example of sublimity that goes all the way back at least to the Roman Stoic, Seneca.[38] And while it could in principle be handled as a textured expanse of sheer immensity, like the sea,[39] for the most part it is not treated this way. It is not the relative emptiness of outer space that struck most theorists of its sublimity, but rather its suggestion of rationally ordered perfection. Thus, Moses Mendelssohn, Kant's German predecessor, invokes the 'innumerable legions of stars' as emblematic of 'the immensity of the structure of the world', the

---

[35] *Spectator* no. 489 (Bond 1965 [v.4]:234).   [36] *Essays*, VIII.iii (1969:772).

[37] Guyer (2014:220n120) presents Reid as an outlier in the Anglophone tradition for something like this reason.

[38] See §5 for discussion of this example in Seneca, Mendelssohn, and Kant.

[39] For an example of this possible way of handling the starry night sky – as graphically akin to an expanse of sea – consider the paintings of Vija Celmins.

finely articulated product of 'the divine perfection' (1997:144-5 [1929:I.398-9]). The two examples thus distinguish crucially different traditions on the sublime in nature: the Anglophone tradition tends to see the immensity of nature as formless and undifferentiated, while the German rationalist tradition (chiefly in its development by Mendelssohn) sees it as infinitely articulated and ordered.

The significance of this difference between the examples of the sea and the starry night sky can be brought out by considering another stock example of sublimity: Genesis 1.3 – 'And God said, 'Let there be light'; and there was light' – which makes a regular appearance in writing on the sublime going back to Longinus (*On the Sublime* 9.9 [1995:190-1]), and does so full well in the Anglophone tradition, though some were struck that 'the heathen critic' would be so moved by these words.[40] Genesis 1.3 presents sublimity as the product of sheer divine power, and thus effectively as an example of the first sort – somewhat akin to Addison's or Reid's sea, when taken as God's work. Henry Home, Lord Kames, concurs in his 1762 *Elements of Criticism*, that 'it is scarce possible, in fewer words, to convey so clear an image of the infinite power of the Deity'; yet, he avers that

> the sublimity raised by this image is but momentary; and that the mind, unable to support itself in an elevation so much above nature, immediately sinks down into humility and veneration for a being so far exalted above grovelling mortals.   (2005:172)

We cannot have a determinate idea of what it would be to suddenly create light – from the power of one's own thought or speech – when there had been nothing but darkness. We can only make a form of words that suggests such a power, the image of which produces a shock to our thought, but not sustained admiration. Kames blames the sublimity of Genesis for its failure to set us in some determinate orientation – because it invokes sheer, incomprehensible power – which,

---

[40] Reid, *Essays* VIII.iii (1969:771); note also Baillie (Ashfield and de Bolla 1996:93).

since we cannot coherently aspire to it, leaves us cast down and depressed.

Here Kames may have influenced Kant quite profoundly. For although Kant had, in his early work, taken the appreciation of sublimity to be an inherently exhausting affair that could not be sustained for long,[41] he later points in a famous passage to a sublimity of mind that gathers strength the more it is sustained: 'Two things fill the mind with ever new and increasing admiration [*Bewunderung*] and reverence [*Ehrfurcht*] the more often and more steadily one considers them: *the starry heavens above me and the moral law within me*' (CPrR 5:161).[42] We will consider this passage briefly in §3.3, and in greater detail in §5.2. Here, I simply want to note that Kant points to the example of natural sublimity that many would say best triggers ideas of divine creation – the starry night sky – and treats it instead as a stimulus to *reflection*. Perhaps he supposes, with Kames, that ideas of divine creative power are far too notional to grip us for long.[43] Not so with the moral law, some tacit grasp of which is – in Kant's view – at least implicit in every use of common practical reason. As we will see, it is with this constellation of ideas that Kant is able to take sublimity to be absolute greatness, while accepting the general outline of the reflective turn in the Anglophone tradition.

---

[41] See Kant's 1764 *Observations on the Feeling of the Beautiful and Sublime*, where he contends that appreciating the sublime is a 'tiring' affair that 'cannot be enjoyed as long' as the beautiful (2:211).

[42] I made this point about the transition of Kant's thinking on the sublime in Merritt (2012 and 2017); Kant's handling of the starry heavens example in this passage figures as a case of *natural* sublimity that does not fall neatly on either side of his 'mathematical'/'dynamical' division, as I will discuss in §3.

[43] Kant's *Observations* was published about a year after Kames's *Elements*, and if he learned from Kames on this point, it would have been via the 1766 translation-cum-commentary of Christian Garve and J. N. Meinhard. Thus, Kames would have been an early influence on Kant's aesthetics, but not in time to have made an impact on the *Observations* – the influence would have come later, corroborating my point here.

3   The Aesthetic Appreciation of Natural Sublimity

My aim in this section is chiefly expository: to lay out Kant's account of the sublime in the *Critique of the Power of Judgment* as much as possible in its own terms. As we will see, however, the third *Critique*'s Analytic of the Sublime points outside of itself, to a set of concerns about the proper development of human reason – which, for Kant, is ultimately the ethical development of virtue.

3.1   Herder's Charge

The idea that the Analytic of the Sublime is not a closed system, that it relies on essentially moral commitments about value, is not a new interpretive claim.[44] But its philosophical implications are, and have long been, controversial.

The worry is that Kant's account of the sublime is ultimately 'self-regarding': we *seem* to be awestruck by the greatness of nature, when in fact we are awestruck by ourselves. The charge can be traced at least as far back as J. G. Herder's 1800 *Kalligone*. The Kantian, who sets out with a conception of sublimity as absolute greatness and accepts a division between sensible and supersensible orders of being, infers that nothing sensible can, strictly speaking, be sublime. That much is straightforwardly presented in Kant's texts, as we saw in §2. However, Herder takes it to have two possible implications. First, if *what is* sublime is absolutely great and can thus only be something supersensible, then our appreciation of it cannot run through channels of sensible affection: there can be no *felt* appreciation of sublimity by Kantian lights. Second, Herder contends, if *what is* sublime must lie in our supersensible personality, and if the principle of personhood is nothing other than the moral law, then any apparent attraction to natural

---

[44] Indeed, Brady (2013:70) dubs it the 'standard interpretation' of Kant on the sublime – though instances of it are quite varied in tenor and details: cf., e.g., Crowther (1989:19–37), Schaper (1992:384–5), Murdoch (1999 [1959]:263–4), Guyer (1993:27–47 and 2005:224–30), Merritt (2012 and 2017), and Rayman (2012). (In contrast to Brady, Rayman presents it as the underdog.)

sublimity must be redescribed as a flush of pride in our own moral perfection.[45]

On the face of it, Kant's text offers a ready line of reply on both fronts. First, Kant argues that we enjoy natural sublimity through a special sort of *aesthetic* – rather than cognitive – judgement: we appreciate sublimity in the register of feeling. He describes the appreciation of natural sublimity as involving a mixed state of mind, one that may be likened to 'a vibration, i.e., to a rapidly alternating repulsion from and attraction to one and the same object' (5:258; see also Anth 7:243).[46] How can this attraction and repulsion be held together in a single experience? The attraction and the repulsion, Kant answers, stem from distinct resources of mind. The repulsion is rooted in our nature as sensible beings: what figures as a threat to our physical existence, or at least to our sense of orientation and readiness to move about in self-perspicuous ways, is unpleasant. But this is comingled with an attraction that is not based in sensible affection at all, but rather in a certain feeling for our own power of reason. Kant's account of the 'aesthetic' status of our appreciation of natural sublimity relies on the idea that there are genuine feelings proper to our *rational* nature, as we will see in §3.2–3 – although what these feelings are, and how they are possible, will be not be considered until §4.

The second facet of Herder's charge is more difficult to address. As a basic interpretive point, it is certainly correct that the absolute greatness that Kant contends can only be found in our own minds –

---

[45] Herder structures his commentary on Kant's Analytic of the Sublime as a series of 'questions' (quotations from Kant's texts) and 'answers'; this two-pronged complaint emerges as Herder's answer to Kant's starting conception of sublimity as absolute greatness (Herder 1998:880–1). On Herder's account of the sublime in *Kalligone*, see Zuckert (2003). Budd (2002:84–9) offers a contemporary version of Herder's complaint; Brady (2013:45, 67–89) frames her interpretation of Kant as a rejoinder to it.

[46] This is by no means a unique feature of Kant's account of the sublime. For a vivid, and early, description of the experience of natural sublimity as mixed in this way, see John Dennis's account of his hike in the Alps: 'The sense of all this produc'd different motions in me, viz., a delightful Horrour, a terrible Joy, and at the same time, that I was infinitely pleas'd, I trembled' (Dennis 1693:134).

not in any object in nature – must ultimately be understood in terms of the absolute, or incomparable, worth we possess as persons (G 4:434). Properly interpreted, however, this underwrites no implications of moralistic self-satisfaction. For Herder misses the distinctive modality of Kant's version of the reflective turn: Kant does not claim that the apprehension of natural immensity leads us to become aware of powers of mind that are already perfect and require no further cultivation.[47] Rather, he argues that the apprehension of natural immensity puts us in mind of the essential task of being human, which is ultimately and most fundamentally to cultivate moral virtue as the realisation or completion of our rational nature. Kant takes virtue to be an ideal that can only be conceived in pure thought, through the moral law: we can neither presume to meet it in the flesh, nor surmise it in the intimacy of introspection. The result, on Kant's view, is something on the order of a strengthened commitment to the proper *calling* of the human being, the rational animal. In §3.4 we will see how this line of thought emerges in the course of the Analytic of the Sublime.

Yet even if Herder's complaints are readily resolved with careful attention to Kant's texts, he nevertheless puts his finger on a lingering discomfort with Kant's version of the reflective turn. Many will be inclined to think of nature as having a value independently of us, and will want an account of our enjoyment of natural sublimity that leaves us looking out at it, and not in at ourselves.[48] And many will be inclined to think that aesthetic and moral value ought not to be confused, and will want to reject the Kantian idea that our appreciation of natural sublimity is underpinned by some underlying interest in morality. To understand why these are not available options for Kant, we will need to consider his logocentrism about value (i.e. the idea that there is no value in the world independently of reason), and his methodological commitment to undertake philosophical inquiry resolutely

---

[47] As we find in John Baillie's account: see §2.2.1.

[48] Cochrane (2012:135) argues that this is truer to the phenomenology of those experiences.

from the human standpoint. In the final section of the Element (§5), I will show how these commitments shape Kant's account in deep ways, and bear on his complex relation to Stoic sources on the sublime.

3.2 The Aesthetic Judgement of Reflection

Let's begin with the idea that we appreciate natural sublimity in the register of feeling. Kant explains this point by saying that we enjoy sublimity through a certain sort of *aesthetic* judgement. Thus, we will begin by pinpointing what sort of aesthetic judgement this is, by locating it in a wider taxonomy of judgement.

We can understand Kant's idea of *aesthetic* judgement by considering it against its contrast class, *logical* judgement. For the most part, logical judgements determine a given representation under a concept (CJ 5:211); the given representation may be singular (an intuition), or general (another concept). *This is a chair* expresses a determination of the first sort, and *chairs are artefacts* expresses a determination of the second sort.[49] Aesthetic judgements, by contrast, do not determine representations under concepts, but rather express the relation of a given representation to feeling – pleasure or pain – in the *subject* (CJ 5:203). Since feeling plays no role in the determination of objects, aesthetic judgements are essentially non-cognitive.[50]

---

[49] Kant indicates that teleological judgements concerning the objective purposiveness of nature – the topic of the Second Part of the third *Critique* – are 'reflecting' logical judgements (FI 20:221), or cognitive judgements that are 'aimed' at concepts rather than based on them (see CJ 5:209).

[50] Kant distinguishes *sensation* (e.g., of sound, colour, and so forth) from *feeling*: sensation does, while feeling does not, have a role to play in empirical knowledge of objects (CJ 5:206, FI 20:224). Here, and elsewhere, Kant notes the ambiguity in the term 'aesthetic' (FI 20:221-2; cf. A21/B35-6n) when taken to refer to any affection of the subject. The Greek αἴσθησις refers to sense perception; Kant draws from this root meaning in the first *Critique*'s Transcendental Aesthetic, which is concerned with the contribution that sensibility makes to empirical knowledge of nature. But in the third *Critique* 'aesthetic' designates a certain sort of judgement that has its 'determining ground' in a *feeling* of pleasure or pain (FI 20:224).

Any aesthetic judgement is an expression of an immediate like or dislike, in relation to some given representation. In finding some tea delightful, a feeling of pleasure is bound up with the sensible presentation of the tea. But this is an 'aesthetic judgment *of sense*', which Kant distinguishes from his genuine quarry: the 'aesthetic judgment *of reflection*' (FI 20:224).[51] I like this tea, and others might as well: but the liking is not *necessary* – it could be otherwise, and there is no robust sense in which anyone else 'ought' to like this tea as I do. An aesthetic judgement *of reflection*, by contrast, carries a claim to 'universal validity and necessity' (FI 20:225). The liking that is involved cannot, therefore, be rooted in contingent facts about the subject's physical constitution. What, then, is the basis of the pleasure that is involved?

As we set about answering this question, let us first note that Kant takes there to be two varieties of aesthetic judgement of reflection: the judgement of taste through which we appreciate *beauty*, and the judgement concerning the *sublime*.[52] And while there are important differences between them, a general story holds about the nature and source of the pleasure they involve. To tell this story, we need to elaborate more on their shared features.

Both varieties of aesthetic judgement of reflection are *singular*, since both express satisfaction in the sensible presentation of a particular – *this* beautiful shell, *this* sublime mountain view (CJ

---

[51] Kant draws the distinction in these terms in FI (20:224); in the published third *Critique* he speaks of 'aesthetic reflective judgments' (e.g., at CJ 5:266), and avoids casting the liking we have for 'the agreeable' as any kind of aesthetic *judgement* at all. Perhaps this is because the readiness to find things agreeable or disagreeable belongs to rational and non-rational animals alike (CJ 5:210) – and non-rational animals do not *judge*. However, there is still scope for Kant to clarify that, in a self-conscious rational being, the appreciation of what is agreeable or disagreeable is a take on how things are, and therefore fittingly designated as an aesthetic *judgement* of sense.

[52] Kant accordingly divides the Critique of the Aesthetic Power of Judgment (the First Part of the third *Critique*) into the Analytic of the Beautiful (§§1–22, 5: 203–44) and the Analytic of the Sublime (§§23–9, 5:244–78). The sections that remain in the First Part (§§30–60 5:279–356) chiefly concern the appreciation of beauty, and its wider philosophical implications – not the sublime.

5:244). As *aesthetic* judgements, they involve no determinate concepts: 'beautiful' and 'sublime' are not functioning as predicates,
and the judgements make no cognitive claim. Further, our liking
for both the beautiful and the sublime is disinterested: the liking is
neither based on a gratification of the senses, nor an esteem for
what is good or useful for some purpose.[53] And so both judgements
'profess to be universally valid in regard to every subject', inasmuch as they are expressed in a liking of the right sort (5:244). This
particular sort of liking cannot be one that is rooted in contingent
facts about the subject's physical constitution[54] – including facts
about it that are normal in the species, such as the desire for society
and the drive for self-preservation that Burke invoked to explain
our enjoyment of beauty and sublimity.[55] The liking, Kant maintains, can only draw from what is necessarily constitutive of us
inasmuch as we possess a cognitive capacity at all.[56]

In making this last point, Kant describes the distinctive liking as
a satisfaction in the amenability of the singular representation to
'the **faculty of concepts** of the understanding or of reason, as
promoting' it (CJ 5:244). To understand this remark, we need to
clarify some terminological issues. When Kant draws basic divi-
sions in human cognitive powers, he often sets out with
a fundamental distinction between singular and general representation (intuition and concept), which he maps onto a distinction
between sensibility and understanding. The 'understanding' in this
broad sense is the 'faculty of concepts'.[57] Further, as the above

---

[53] See Kant's account of the disinterestedness of the judgement of taste (CJ §2–5 5:
204–11), which he here extends to include the judgement concerning the
sublime ('both please for themselves', CJ 5:244).

[54] That is a 'pathologically conditioned satisfaction' (CJ 5:209).   [55] See §2.2.2.

[56] In the first two *Critiques*, Kant claims to isolate what is necessarily constitutive of
any cognitive capacity at all, whether or not such a capacity is embodied in
a creature such as us. Thus, the table of categories is meant to be exhaustively
constitutive of any finite capacity for theoretical cognition (A79/B105); and the
moral law is meant to be necessarily constitutive of any cognitive exercise of
practical, or will-determining, reason (CPrR 5:19–22). These claims are not uncon-
troversial, but it lies beyond the scope of my work here to try to defend them.

[57] A126; Anth (7:196–7); as well as JL (9:36) and Wiener Logik (24:806, 846) both in
Kant (1992).

quotation indicates, there are different sorts of concepts. Concepts of understanding are rules for the determination of phenomenal objects in the domain of nature. Concepts of reason are *ideas*: concepts that 'go beyond the possibility of experience' (A320/B377).[58] More will need to be said about ideas of reason as we take a closer look at the judgement concerning the sublime in §3.3. For now, I simply want to note that understanding and reason alike are *cognitive* capacities. Pure concepts of the understanding – the categories – form the basis of a battery of substantive principles that spell out what it is to be a phenomenal object, an entity in the domain of nature. The story about ideas of reason is more complicated, since the role of ideas in the *theoretical* employment of reason is simply to regulate inquiry. But reason is a cognitive capacity in its *practical* exercise: it is itself the source of a principle with substantive, objective purport – the moral law.[59] This is the principle by which the self-determined freedom of a rational being, or supersensible personhood, is made actual.[60] Thus, the liking involved in the aesthetic judgement of reflection is effectively a function of our *cognitive* constitution, broadly construed.[61] The enjoyment we take in the beautiful shell or the

[58] Understanding (in the narrow sense) and reason (also in a narrow sense) are elements of what Kant calls the 'higher cognitive faculty'; a complication here is that Kant sometimes refers to this whole package – the higher cognitive faculty as such – as understanding in the broad sense (see A131/B169; Anth 7:196–7), and sometimes as reason, again in some broad sense (consider A835/B863).

[59] This is the significance of Kant's deeming the moral law an 'a priori *synthetic* practical proposition' (G 4:420).

[60] Theoretical cognition 'merely *determines*' its object, 'which must be supplied from elsewhere' (i.e., a given, sensible object), whereas practical cognition does *not merely* determine its object but *also* makes 'it actual' (Bix–x). Practical knowledge is efficacious – it brings its object, the good (CPrR 5: 57–8), into being. By Kant's lights, the good is fundamentally autonomy, and thus the self-determination of rational beings.

[61] On reason as a cognitive capacity in its practical exercise, consider the many references to practical *cognition* in the ethical works (G 4:389, 390, 392, 393, 403, 409, 411, 420, 447; CPrR 5:20, 38, 46) – and remarks that present reason as a cognitive capacity in its practical (will-determining) exercise (CPrR 5:89, 121). Cf. CJ (5:167); however, he begins there by identifying reason as a cognitive capacity, so that his ensuing remark that the first *Critique* (but not the second)

sublime mountain view is a satisfaction in its amenability to us as creatures capable of knowing.

But while we enjoy beauty with unadulterated liking, our appreciation of sublimity is bivalent. Although a pleasurable attraction must govern this state of mind as long as we are moved to sustain it (see CJ 5:220), disagreeable aversion is an essential ingredient. To account for this, we need to consider the differences between beauty and sublimity. Kant takes beautiful objects to be – paradigmatically – bounded, articulated, organised wholes: they present themselves as eminently comprehensible, but we do not actually comprehend them (in the judgement of taste) under concepts of the understanding: 'natural beauty ... carries with it a purposiveness in its form, through which the object seems as it were to be predetermined for our power of judgement' (5:245). Natural sublimity, however, does not announce itself as comprehensible – quite the contrary. Sublimity requires 'a formless object insofar as **limitlessness** is represented in it' (5:244), which assaults, and overwhelms, our capacity to comprehend it. Hence, Kant contends that pleasure in the sublime is 'very different in kind' from pleasure in the beautiful. For the beautiful

> *directly* brings with it a feeling of the promotion of life ... while the latter (the feeling of the sublime) is a pleasure that arises only *indirectly*, being generated, namely, by the feeling of a momentary inhibition of the vital powers and the immediately following and all the more powerful outpouring of them. (5:245; emphasis added)

Kant identifies the pleasure we take in beauty with 'a feeling of the promotion of life' – that is, with a direct, or concomitant, delight in its enlivening of our cognitive capacities.[62] His second point,

---

is concerned with the 'cognitive faculty' is evidently restricted to *theoretical* cognition of phenomenal objects.

[62] Kant's suggestion that the enjoyment we take in beauty is a certain 'feeling of the promotion of life' appears to have roots in Meier's development of Baumgarten's aesthetics. As noted in §2.3, Baumgarten takes beauty to be the 'perfection of sensible cognition'; he lists the 'life' of such cognition as the final aspect of this perfection. But Baumgarten never completed

however, is not that our enjoyment of the sublime has nothing to do with the enlivening of our cognitive capacities. Rather, it is that this pleasure arises *indirectly*, so that an assault on cognitive powers of one sort invigorates cognitive powers of another sort.[63] To fill in this sketch, we must now consider the aesthetic judgement concerning the sublime in greater detail.

3.3 Sublimity of Size and of Power

Kant's introduction to the Analytic of the Sublime (CJ §23) moves from what is generally true about the aesthetic judgement of reflection to what is specifically true of those judgements which concern the sublime. Thus, the liking involved in judgements concerning the sublime is a satisfaction in the amenability of a sensible representation to the 'faculty of concepts' – where this is specified as the faculty of concepts of reason, or *ideas* of the supersensible. Kant then divides his exposition of judgements concerning the sublime into those that express satisfaction in greatness of size, and those that express satisfaction in greatness of power, calling them the 'mathematical' and 'dynamical' sublime respectively. This division, as we will see, aligns with the different roles that ideas of reason play in theoretical and practical cognition, respectively (CJ 5:247).

The standard way to read the Analytic of the Sublime is to take the division between the mathematical and the dynamical sublime to be sharp and deep, on the grounds that the one involves a satisfaction of reason in its *theoretical* capacity, and the other a satisfaction of reason in its *practical* capacity. However, it is surely possible to recognise that mathematical and dynamical

---

Aesthetica - and it was left to Meier to develop an account of this 'life'. For an exposition of Meier on this point, see Guyer (2014:331, 337–40).

[63] I.e., an assault on imagination invigorates reason. Lyotard (1994:188) points to CJ 5:269 as evidence that the sublime also ultimately 'enlarges' the imagination. This line of interpretation, while not entirely implausible, would require development through an account of aesthetic ideas and artistic sublimity – reconstructive work that lies outside of my aims here.

sublimity are distinguished in this way, and still reject any conclusion that mathematical and dynamical sublimity must be mutually exclusive by Kant's lights. For one thing, sublimity of size and power are not, in their concrete manifestations, often neatly separable from one another. A swelling surf is both massive and crushing; a desert threatens death with its vastness; a lintel at Stonehenge looms overhead and suggests, with that, the prodigious strength that laid it there. Almost any *example* of natural sublimity works on us in both registers at once. Consider Kant's catalogue of dynamical sublimity: 'Bold, overhanging, as it were threatening cliffs, thunder clouds towering up into the heavens, bringing with them flashes of lightening and crashes of thunder, volcanoes with their all-destroying violence, hurricanes with the devastation they leave behind, the boundless ocean set into a rage, a lofty waterfall on a mighty river, etc.' (CJ 5:261) – these all appear to be candidates for dynamical-cum-mathematical sublimity. Even Kant's famous 'starry heavens' example is not handled as a case of straight-up mathematical sublimity. It certainly underscores the vastness, and so the mathematical sublimity, of the heavens: 'an unbounded magnitude with worlds upon worlds and systems of systems, and moreover into the unbounded times of their periodic motion, their beginning and their duration' (CPrR 5:162). But Kant then suggests that the view of this vastness 'annihilates, as it were, my importance as an *animal creature*, which after it has been for a short time provided with vital force (one knows not how) must give back to the planet (a mere speck in the universe) the matter from which it came' (5:162).[64] Nature figures as a force that ultimately overwhelms the form of any living species, reclaiming the matter in which it had realised itself.

Of course, while any particular experience of natural sublimity is liable to tap into both mathematical and dynamical modes at once, there could still be no deeper, or more systematic, account of their unity. But Kant's texts suggest otherwise. As we will see, the fact

[64] The 'starry heavens' passage may still be atypical among Kant's writings on the sublime for other reasons, as I note at the end of §5.

that a person is able to revel in such manifestations – whether greatness of size, of power, or both at once – depends, on Kant's view, upon the development of her capacity for *moral* feeling, and commitment to essentially moral ends (CJ 5:265). Although this point becomes gradually more *explicit* as Kant's account proceeds from the mathematical to the dynamical sublime, it should hold across the board. One way to see that is to recall that we enjoy *natural* sublimity in an *aesthetic* judgement, and thus cannot put into play any morally determinate idea of the good. If so, then (contra the standard reading) the dynamical sublime should in principle be no 'closer' to ethical concerns than the mathematical. They may then be equally dependent on the subject's background commitment to moral ends. I will make my case for that claim in §3.4, once we have considered the mathematical and dynamical sublime each in turn.

3.3.1 The Mathematical Sublime

Kant's account begins with the 'nominal definition' of the sublime that we have already considered in §2: 'We call **sublime** that which is **absolutely great**' (CJ 5:248). It is crucial to recognise that this may hold for mathematical and dynamical sublimity alike, since the presentation of greatness may be either of size or of power. But if we now ask *how* great something is, we call for a measurement to be made.[65] To do this, we need to specify how many iterations of some given unit the thing is: this Kant calls the 'logical estimation' of magnitude (5:251). Since the iteration of units can proceed infinitely, measurement in this sense has no limits. We can in turn ask how big the unit of measure itself is; and this question can only be answered by considering it in comparison against something else, or as so many units of measure of some other sort. Thus, our ability to think and 'estimate' spatial magnitudes is essentially comparative, and analogical. If we are trying to think

---

[65] While we can measure all sorts of things (e.g. heat in degrees Celsius, or force in horsepower), Kant is here concerned with the measurement of spatial dimension, or *size*.

of how great a solar system is, we might relate it to the width of one of its planets; and we can iterate these moves to estimate the breadth of the Milky Way – or back in the other direction, to estimate how small, say, the polio virus is (5:250, 256–7).[66]

But the *aesthetic* estimation of magnitude works differently: it is the immediate grasp of magnitude 'in an intuition' (CJ 5:251) – in effect, how great something strikes you as being, as you take it in by eye. And while logical estimation of magnitude knows no limits, the aesthetic estimation does: for certain things, from certain perspectives, will prove too large to take in at a single glance. Mathematical sublimity arises at this breaking point. Quite obviously, where one stands in relation to the thing in question is crucial for an experience of sublimity. Kant explains this by citing Nicholas Savary's observation from his 1787 *Lettres sur l'Égypte*, that one only gets the 'full emotional effect of the magnitude of the pyramids' if one stands in a kind of sweet spot: one must not stand so far that the whole pyramid easily registers as a continuous form in a single glance, and one must stand so close that one only takes in a mass that consumes even the periphery of one's vision, so that one has no sense of boundaries at all (5:252). Rather, one needs to stand where one will try to have the whole thing in one's sights, but just fail. Or as Kant puts it: 'the eye requires some time to complete its apprehension' – sensible uptake – 'from the base level to the apex, but during this time the former always partly fades before the imagination has taken in the latter, and the comprehension is never complete' (5:252).

Now we need to consider why this failure of sensible comprehension should appeal to us as rational beings, and thus arouse

---

[66] Thus Kant says that the logical estimation of magnitude of any sensible particular – no matter how great or how small – requires us to seek a standard of measure 'outside' it; but the consideration of *absolute* magnitude requires us to seek a standard 'merely within' the thing in question (5:250). The first point is relatively clear, and follows as a corollary from the idea that any sensible particular can only be of 'relative' greatness. The second point is not so clear, and seems to be little more than a placeholder for the idea of a standard of evaluation that is internal to personhood itself (the moral law).

a feeling of the sublime. At this failure of sensible comprehension, Kant contends, 'the mind hears in itself the voice of reason, which requires totality for all given magnitudes ... and hence comprehension in **one** intuition' (CJ 5:254). To understand this, we need to elaborate further on Kant's conception of reason. In the first *Critique*, Kant notes the logical definition of reason as the 'faculty of making mediated inferences' (A299/B355) – which, when the 'real use' of reason is at issue, is a matter of determining dependence relations within a body of substantive cognitive claims. Reason seeks coherence, and is after systems: the paradigmatic expression of rational cognition is a systematic whole of cognition established according to a priori principles, or *science* (MFNS 4: 467–8). So it is the 'voice of reason' that calls, quite generally, for the grasp of things as a whole, or comprehension. Reason even calls for us to think of an infinitely progressing series as a whole: 'it demands a **presentation** for all members of a progressively increasing numerical series, and does not exempt from this requirement even the infinite (space and past time), but rather makes it unavoidable for us to think of it (in the judgment of common reason) as **given entirely** (in its totality)' (CJ 5:254).

These remarks hark back to the First Antinomy of the *Critique of Pure Reason*, which demonstrated distinct cognitive pressures to think of the cosmos as being, on the one hand, bounded in time and space (in the thesis position), and, on the other hand, infinite in time and space (in the antithesis).[67] Yet both sides, Kant explains, stake cognitive claims about the world as a whole, and thus surreptitiously take the infinite series of appearances to be itself *given* as a totality. Here the fraudulent employment of reason needs to be carefully distinguished from its legitimate role in empirical enquiry. If we suppose that nature is the phenomenal order of being, we conceive of it as a totality of appearances: this is an idea of reason, since 'the sum total of all appearances' could not itself ever be given in experience. The appearances, which are infinite, form a whole. We have no cognitive access to this totality –

---

[67] A426–34/B454–62, A517–23/B545–51.

that is one of the lessons of the First Antinomy – and yet we need this idea in order to conceive of nature as a law-governed whole, and thereupon to pursue, on perfectly firm epistemic ground, empirical natural science.[68] The fraudulent inference of the Antinomy is to take the rational imperative governing empirical inquiry – *comprehend the whole!* – as the basis for claims about the objective conditions of the world as it is in itself.

With this in mind, let us recapitulate the pyramid example and draw out its result. When we stand in the sweet spot, our efforts at a comprehensive uptake of the thing in the senses (*comprehensio aesthetica*, CJ 5:254) fail. But this very struggle, and failure, to comprehend the thing in the senses puts us in mind of another power of mind to conceive, in pure thought, of what can never be met with in the senses. The idea of nature as the sum total of appearances would seem to be the relevant conception here. For Kant says that this rational idea is 'presupposed as the substratum of the intuition of the world as mere appearance' (5:255): the idea underlies the effort to relate appearances according to necessary principles to form a coherent system of experience. That is its legitimate role in regulating empirical cognition. Yet this rational idea concerns the *absolute* totality of the *essentially relational* order of appearances: hence, Kant recalls here the lesson of the Antinomy, that it is 'a self-contradictory concept' (5:255) – it is self-contradictory *as* a concept, as a general representation that claims objective purport. Nevertheless, Kant contends that the bare power to conceive of this absolute totality must 'surpass ... every standard of sense' (5:255), and that the presentation of mathematical

---

[68] Nature as such, taken 'in the material sense' – in its concrete actuality – is conceived as the 'sum total of appearances'; we can have no cognitive access to this whole except through the articulation of nature as a law-governed whole, through a system of synthetic a priori principles of the possibility of experience (the principles of pure understanding). These principles yield comprehension of nature as such, though only with regard to the conditions of its possibility, and thus in the 'formal' sense. For this distinction between 'material' and 'formal' senses of nature, see Transcendental Deduction §26 (B163-5) and *Prolegomena* §36 (4:318-20).

sublimity in nature is thereby emblematic of a certain superiority of reason over sensibility.

It is not, however, entirely clear why we should enjoy this. What figures as sublime in nature arouses efforts of sensible comprehension that fail. That failure is presumably disagreeable: here we have the negative, or repellent, aspect of the bivalent judgement of the sublime. This failure purportedly arouses a calling of mind to 'overstep the limits of sensibility' (5:255). Is this meant to be the basis of our *enjoyment* of the natural immensity in question? It is not obvious that, by Kant's lights, it should be. After all, Kant takes himself to have demonstrated the fraudulence of this calling in the Antinomies – at least where the empirical, and theoretical, employment of reason is at issue. Anyone who has absorbed the lessons of the Antinomies should only be pained by such reminders of our liability to fall into such metaphysical 'enthusiasm' or *Schwärmerei*. What we enjoy, rather, is a feeling of an empowerment of the rational mind to overstep these boundaries *legitimately*, 'from another (practical) point of view' (5:255). We will return to this point when we consider the unity of the mathematical and dynamical sublime in §3.4.

At this point, Kant can only conclude that what is absolutely great must have something to do with the supersensible power of reason: for the failure of sensible comprehension points to our capacity to conceive in pure thought of what can never be present to us in the senses. And while there may be some sense in which nature as the sum total of appearances will always be 'greater than' any given appearance, Kant's point is rather that true sublimity lies in some proper self-determination of reason. He gets there by showing how natural immensity can stimulate a palpable recognition of the limits of our sensible capacities, and lead to a certain feeling for our rational capacity as unlimited by what is, or can be, given to us in the senses. Inasmuch as the rational capacity is unconditioned by the sensible order, it must in some sense be self-determined. But this is still a placeholder. Although Kant conceives of sublimity as absolute greatness throughout his account, the greatness at issue is only initially – and only seemingly – an absolute greatness of size. The sense of greatness at issue expands, in the course of Kant's Analytic of the Sublime, from its root sense pertaining to size to a broader sense pertaining to value. This transition is mostly brought about in the account of the dynamical sublime.

3.3.2 The Dynamical Sublime

The dynamical sublime concerns the presentation of absolute greatness of power in nature. Of course, nothing in nature can be absolutely great in power, just as nothing can be absolutely great in size – at least if we conceive of nature as the phenomenal order, and so a relation of appearances. In both cases, what is sensibly present must *figure as* absolutely great. In the case of the mathematical sublime, Kant can rely on a quasi-mechanical story to make the point: a sensible presentation figures as absolutely great when one cannot hold it together as a whole, in a single intuition. The sensible immensity which we struggle, but fail, to take in is judged as 'unsuitable for our faculty of presentation, and as it were doing violence to our imagination, but is nevertheless judged all the more sublime for that' (5:245; see also 5:259, 260). But dynamical sublimity cannot figure as absolutely great in this way, since there is no striving, but failing, to take something in: we might simply see the twister on the horizon, or the snake lifting smoothly up from its coil.[69] Thus, we need to consider the aspects of the judgement more closely, both in regards to what it shares with mathematical sublimity and how it differs.

Both modes of the aesthetic judgement of the sublime are supposed to involve the relation of a sensible presentation of a particular, through the imagination, to reason. The appreciation of mathematical sublimity relates a sensible representation to reason in its role in theoretical cognition, whereas the

---

[69] Burke mentions the sublimity of small, poisonous beasts (as noted in §2.2.2), which led to my snake example here; and while the twister *is* immense, seeing it off on the horizon wouldn't trigger the breakdown of imagination that Kant postulates in the mathematical sublime.

appreciation of dynamical sublimity relates a sensible representation to reason in its role as the higher **'faculty of desire'**
(CJ 5:247) – i.e., to reason in its role as the determining ground
of the will in practical cognition. Thus, the distinction between
mathematical and dynamical sublimity tracks the distinction
between the theoretical and the practical employment of reason.
Next, both judgements count as *aesthetic* judgements of reflection because they do not involve the application of a concept or
idea to the particular, but rather a pleasurable *feeling*. And both
count as aesthetic judgements *of reflection* because this feeling
concerns the 'purposiveness' of the sensible representation for
one's own cognitive powers – and specifically for reason. So we
like the sensible particular with some sense of its being 'for' us, as
rational beings.

We have already noted (§3.2) that the aesthetic appreciation of
sublimity is necessarily bivalent. While Kant suggests that this can
be explained, in general terms, by noting the 'contrapurposiveness'
of the sensible particular for the faculty of imagination, in fact that
gloss holds straightforwardly only for the mathematical sublime.[70]
For the sensible presentation of nature's might will not obviously
bring the imagination to a breaking point. Nevertheless, it will
require a visceral presentation of a power that could crush and
obliterate one's existence in living flesh and blood: booming
sounds, sensations of impact, visual cues of swiftness, blinding
light, and impenetrable dark. Quite like Burke, Kant contends
that the dynamical sublimity will draw its negative, repelling aspect
from the arousal of feelings associated with self-preservation:
I must have a sense of an overwhelming power, but yet recognise
my own real safety if I am to soak up these sensations rather than
flee (CJ 5:261).[71] Unlike Burke, however, Kant does not think that
the principle of our *enjoyment* of natural sublimity of power lies
simply in recognising one's own real safety. For Kant this is merely

---

[70] This is how he puts the point in his general introduction to the Analytic of the
Sublime, however, which would otherwise suggest that he takes it to hold for
mathematical and dynamical sublimity alike: see CJ §23 (5:245).
[71] Burke (1990:47 and 121–2).

a necessary precondition: and thus the enjoyment is not – as it is for Burke – to be understood as a merely negative delight, an agreeableness that follows simply as a relief from stress or pain.[72] For Kant, by contrast, the enjoyment expresses a positive attraction *to* something.

Dynamical sublimity offers a presentation of immense natural power that challenges our default sense of what is worth going after, what is valuable. Our enjoyment in natural sublimity is ultimately to be explained in terms of an interest in a standard of *goodness* that is proper to us as rational beings. This transition is made in the following:

> [I]n our aesthetic judgment nature is appreciated [*beurtheilt*] as sublime not insofar as it arouses fear, but rather because it calls forth our power [*Kraft*] (which is not part of nature) to regard these things about which we are concerned (worldly goods,[73] health and life) as trivial [*klein*], and hence to regard its might [*Macht*] (to which we are, to be sure, subjected in regard to these things) as not the sort of dominion over ourselves and our authority to which we would have to bow if it came down to our highest principles and their affirmation or abandonment.　　(CJ 5:262; translation modified)

Whatever worldly goods one has, and even one's health and life, could be taken away in a flash of nature's might. Ultimately, we are without any means to resist: we will die, and our bodies return to dust. Moreover, to whatever extent we win the material and social goods we go after, and whether we have even good health and the continuance of life, is not fully up to us: this is nature's dominion over us. But how can we regard worldly goods, health and life, as

---

[72] Indeed, it is this feature of Burke's account that leaves it without obvious resources to account for our interest in natural sublimity – beyond, perhaps, its providing a thrill, or relief from the tedium of bourgeois life (akin to the account of the sublimity of tragedy offered by Abbé Du Bos, as discussed by Guyer [2014:79–83]). Perhaps it is because Burke recognised this that he offered a second explanation, that we enjoy the sublime for the *exercise* it provides to the mind (see §2.2.2).

[73] The German simply has *Güter*, but the implication of this usage is *worldly* goods (Cambridge translation) or property (Pluhar).

'small' or 'trivial' (*klein*) in a contest against 'our highest principles'? We must recognise some other standard of value, 'a unit
against which everything in nature is small' (CJ 5:261). This standard must lie in our freedom from the dominion that nature exerts
over us as merely *animal* beings. With this, Kant shifts the discussion from an absolute greatness of size and power that can only be
apparent in nature to a principle of unconditioned *value* that is
supposed to be real in us.

Without an active appreciation of the good that can only be
conceived in pure thought, through the moral law, a person will
only be repulsed by the threatening immensity of nature (CJ
5:265). One must conceive of oneself as a *person*, and see this
personality – one's rational nature – as something that can only
be realised and cultivated through self-determined choice and
action.[74] The idea is not that one would need to have grasped
the supersensible principle of one's rational nature explicitly, *in
abstracto*; but rather that one must have grasped it concretely, in
knowing what to do and how to live. This involves cultivating the
readiness to be *moved* by one's recognition of what morality
requires of one, situation by situation. Hence, Kant insists that
our enjoyment of the natural sublimity 'has its foundation in
human nature' – that is, in what is proper to us as embodied
rational beings – and specifically 'in the predisposition to the
feeling for (practical) ideas, i.e., to that which is moral' (CJ
5:265).[75] In §4 we will examine the feeling that expresses our

---

[74] Thus, Kant had said at the outset that one stands to appreciate 'the wide ocean,
enraged by storms' – something horrifying – as *sublime* only if one has
'already ... filled the mind with all sorts of ideas, [... namely,] ideas that
contain a higher purposiveness' (CJ 5:246).

[75] Kant says in this passage (CJ §29) that enjoyment of natural sublimity requires
a certain 'cultivation [*Cultur*]' that the enjoyment of beauty does not require
(5:265). Doran (2015:262) misinterprets this to mean that Kant takes the sublime to be culturally relative, which he then finds to be inconsistent with the
universality claimed in any aesthetic judgement of reflection. There is no such
problem in Kant's account. The term *Cultur* here means 'cultivation' of given
resources of mind (i.e. of 'talents', in Kant's technical sense: for such usage see
G 4:393, Refl 404 [14:163]), which is part of a person's formation or *Bildung*: see
CPR (A709–10/B737–8) for this explanation of the term. Thus, what Kant is

appreciation of natural sublimity (*admiration*), and how Kant distinguishes it from the genuine moral feeling of *respect*.

3.4 *The Sublime Human* Bestimmung

As we have seen, Kant's account belongs to a 'reflective' tradition on the sublime, whereby natural immensity provides an occasioning stimulus that allows us to revel in some prodigious power of our own minds. Earlier proponents of the reflective turn in the Anglophone tradition did not, for the most part, subscribe to a dualism distinguishing sensible and supersensible orders of being. Thus, there is no natural place in such a tradition for a conception of sublimity as *absolute* greatness, since whatever can figure in the phenomenal order can only ever be relatively great. In such a tradition, 'sublime' refers to the arousal of a certain psychological phenomenon with comingled impulses of repulsion and attraction. But Kant supposes that his own account of the sublime rises above empirical psychology, since the pleasurable aspect of the judgement is a function of a certain attraction to one's own essential purposes, or calling, as a rational being (CJ 5:277-8).[76] What I dislike for its lack of amenability to my physical existence, I enjoy for its amenability to the complete picture of what I called to be as a *rational* animal.

The crucial term here – *Bestimmung* – which most basically means 'determination', functions in a special way in this context. Kant alludes to a longstanding eighteenth-century debate about the *Bestimmung des Menschen*, the 'vocation' or 'calling' of the human being.[77] The ancient formula of our kind takes *rational* to

saying here is that our enjoyment of natural sublimity requires some background cultivation of our moral capacity, and particularly of moral feeling.

[76] Kant mentions Burke in this passage, praising his 'fine' psychological observations while condemning his empirical approach as unable to account for the universal validity claimed in an aesthetic judgement of reflection.

[77] The key players were Thomas Abbt and Moses Mendelssohn, debating the merits of Johann Joachim Spalding's 1748 *Betrachtung über die Bestimmung des Menschen*. For discussions of this debate that address its significance for Kant, see Brandt (2003), Kuehn (2009), and di Giovanni (2011).

be our essence or form, distinguishing us from the rest of the animal kingdom; but Kant stresses that this rational nature presents itself as a practical problem, rather than a given endowment – a task, not a fact. A human being is 'an animal endowed with *rational capability* (*animal rationabile*)' and is called to 'make out of himself a *rational animal* (*animal rationale*)' (Anth 7: 321–2). The given endowment needs to be cultivated, and made complete: thus, Kant takes the *Bestimmung* of our species to consist in 'perfection' (Anth 7:322). Although Kant emphasises, in his anthropological writings, that no individual can fulfil this calling – it is a task for the species as a whole – he nevertheless accords a central place to the perfection of the individual in his later ethical writings. In the Doctrine of Virtue in the *Metaphysics of Morals*, Kant divides duties of virtue into what one owes oneself, and what one owes others; these follow, respectively, from the free adoption of the two morally obligatory ends of self-perfection and the happiness of others (MM-DV 6:385). Self-perfection calls for the cultivation of one's capacities, 'the highest of which is the *understanding* as the faculty of concepts' – where this is, once again, construed broadly to include 'concepts having to do with duty' (6:386–7). To make oneself fit for one's own essential rationality is itself a moral obligation, a duty of virtue; and while this is originally, or most basically, a matter of cultivating one's cognitive capacities, it is ultimately a matter of cultivating one's *will* or 'moral way of thinking' (6:387) according to the standard of virtue that is thought through the moral law.

In Kant's account, we appreciate (what we in shorthand call) natural sublimity because it resonates with this vocation in some cognitively indeterminate register of feeling:

> [N]ature is here called sublime merely because it raises the imagination to the point of presenting those cases in which the mind can make palpable [*fühlbar*] to itself the sublimity of its own vocation over nature.   (CJ 5:262; see also 5:264)

Repeatedly, Kant deems this calling sublime: he speaks of the 'sublimity of our moral vocation' (6:50) and the '*feeling of the sublimity* of our own vocation' (6:23 n) in the *Religion*; and of the 'sublimity of our nature (in its vocation)' (5:87) in the second *Critique*. Therefore, what is truly sublime cannot be any given fact of a perfected faculty of reason by Kant's lights, for no such fact can be given to us. Virtue itself is the perfection of our rational nature; and it is an ideal that, for all we know, may never yet have been attained; its manifestation can neither be directly perceived in others, nor introspected in ourselves (MM-DV 6:383, 396, 409; CPrR 5:83). Contra Herder, Kant's reflective turn cannot be a matter of a so-called sublimity of nature leading us to admire an actual perfection within us. At the same time, the governing attraction of the sublime is a commitment to one's own super-sensible personality – a commitment we must undertake *gladly*, if this is to be expressed in some kind of sustained pleasurable feeling. So there must be some kind of confidence in one's in-principle capacity to answer this calling (CJ 5:262), but without any arrogant presumption that one has, or ever will, answer it once and for all.

With this in mind, let us return to the contested question of whether or not Kant means to draw a sharp and deep division between mathematical and dynamical modes of natural sublimity. The standard view is that he does. However, a closer look at how the sublime human *Bestimmung* figures in the Analytic of the Sublime, and particularly in a section that belongs to the exposition of the mathematical sublime (CJ §27), tells against the standard view.

In CJ §27 Kant begins with an account of the feeling of respect: 'The feeling of the inadequacy of our capacity for the attainment of an idea **that is a law for us** is **respect**' (5:257). The 'law' that Kant has in mind right here is evidently not the *moral* law, but rather the regulative principle to seek complete-ness in the determination of the 'sum total of appearances'. The possibility of scientific cognition of material nature requires that we regulate inquiry according to this idea (recall §3.3.1); and yet we can never attain the completeness that it calls for. In the case of the mathematically sublime, a massive object arouses efforts of imagination whereby it 'demonstrates its limits and inadequacy, but at the same time its vocation [*Bestimmung*] for adequately realising that idea as a law' (5:257). The immense object is emblematic of this calling, an imperative over cognitive conduct: *comprehend the whole!* For it suggests a bounded infinity, as if it were the totality of everything that is, the sum total of appearances. And since, in the mathematically sublime, one *fails* to comprehend the whole in a sensible representation, one recognises both the imperative (the 'law') and the inadequacy of one's capacity to attain it. Hence, there is a sense in which respect is the appropriate attitude to take (or feeling to have) towards it.[78] From here, Kant draws a conclusion that he indicates should hold for natural sublimity tout court:

> Thus the feeling of the sublime in nature is respect for our own vocation, which we show to an object in nature through a certain subreption (substitution of a respect for the object instead of for the idea of humanity in our subject), which as it were makes intuitable the superiority of the rational vocation of our cognitive faculty over the greatest faculty of sensibility. (CJ 5:257)[79]

Kant does not expressly limit the scope of this claim to the mathematically sublime. The proper object of respect, he indicates here, is 'humanity' (in this case, that in one's own subject). But what is 'humanity'? For Kant, it is the capacity to freely set ends and act on them: 'The capacity to set oneself an end – any end whatsoever – is what characterises humanity (as distinguished from animality)' (MM-DV 6:392). Now consider that both mathematical and

---

[78] Certain things about Kant's gloss of respect in CJ §27 are jarring in relation to his canonical account of respect in CPrR, which we will consider in §4.1. Crucially, Kant here casts respect *as a feeling of inadequacy*, placing (it seems to me) too strong an emphasis on the negative or repelling aspect of the bivalent feeling.

[79] In the CPR Transcendental Dialectic, 'subreption' is explained as the fallacious hypostatisation of a mere idea of reason (A389, A402, A509/B537, A583/B661; A619/B647); see also Kant's Inaugural Dissertation (2:412). Subreption is not presented as a fallacy in the Analytic of the Sublime, since the judgement at issue is non- cognitive.

dynamical sublimity make an assault on our normal sense of agency. Mathematical sublimity disorients: the difficulty of taking in the immensity in a single presentation leaves one without a clear sense of one's place in the world, and seizes one's readiness to carry on in the normal ways. The point is even stronger in the case dynamical sublimity, which Kant suggests challenges our normal concerns with worldly goods, health, and life (recall CJ 5:262). We are inclined to pursue these things, but they could all be wiped out when nature's force bursts forth. But our *humanity* is not assaulted, if this capacity is realised in the self-determination of the will through the moral law. Thus, Kant says in the above passage that it is appropriate to show something like respect to the large or mighty object in nature, since it provides the occasion to appreciate, through feeling, that we are not subject to its 'dominion' in being what we properly are, as *rational* animals.

Indeed, it is a thought like this that Kant draws upon when he extols the 'sublime and mighty name' of '*Duty!*' in the second *Critique*: the origin of its nobility that 'rejects all kinship with the inclinations ... can be nothing less than what elevates a human being above himself (as part of the sensible world), what connects him with an order of things that only the understanding can think' – connects him, that is, with the supersensible order of '*personality*, that is, freedom and independence from the mechanism of the whole of nature, regarded nevertheless as also a capacity of a being subject to ... pure practical laws given by his own reason' (CPrR 5:86–7). With this we can see that Kant's repeated talk of the *sublimity* of the human vocation is rather literal, at least in a rhetorical framework that places the supersensible order of being 'above' the sensible. We are *called up* to make ourselves fit for our own essential rationality, to claim our status as persons rather than things.[80] Moreover, Kant concludes this rather florid passage with

[80] Kant speaks of 'the sublimity and inner dignity of the command in a duty' (G 4:425): the command, as it were, calls one up to do something, regardless of how one might be otherwise inclined. Yet there is a difference between the very idea of categorical moral requirements and the readiness to heed those requirements, and true sublimity does not consist in merely hearing the call,

reference to the 'second and highest vocation' of the human being (5:87). The remark is a bit puzzling, since in that passage he never says what the first, and presumably 'lower', vocation might be. But his discussion of the morally obligatory end of self-perfection from the Doctrine of Virtue (6:386–7), which I have already sketched above, provides a clue. The perfection proper to 'humanity' in the strict sense must consist first in cultivating the resources of body and mind that will better enable one to freely pursue ends and act on them; Kant says that the 'highest' of these resources (*Vermögen*) is the understanding in the broad sense as 'the faculty of concepts'. Since the understanding so conceived includes concepts of duty, the human vocation must *ultimately* consist in (and its fulfilment be determined by) the cultivation of the will according to the standard of virtue that can only be thought through the moral law. Thus, the fulfilment of the duty of self-perfection consists of cultivating both natural and moral perfections: the first are developed with the setting of discretionary ends, the second with the adoption of the morally obligatory end to care about humanity in one's own person and in others. For this very reason, the natural perfections are dependent upon the moral perfection of virtue, for only through our active, practical commitment to the latter can the former be part of the *good*, or the true calling, of a human being.[81]

but in heeding it. Thus, Kant says that we rightly 'represent a certain sublimity and *dignity* in the person who fulfils all his duties' (G 4:440), and then elaborates that there is no sublimity in a person simply 'insofar as he is *subject* to the moral law', since there is no idea of anything uplifting just in that. There is sublimity in him *first* inasmuch as his own rational nature is the source of the law, and *second* that in heeding its command he transforms himself, making himself (at least in some sense) more properly a *person*.

[81] The 'second and highest' *Bestimmung*, in other words, consists in the cultivation of virtue; but an original, and in some sense more basic, *Bestimmung* consists in the cultivation of cognitive capacities generally. Thus, note the 'original' human *Bestimmung* that consists in progress towards enlightenment and accordingly calls for the appropriate cultivation of cognitive capacities (WIE 8:39); or the 'natural' *Bestimmung* that consists in the 'development of all talents' (Refl 1454 [1778–89] 15:635–6) – which would include the natural dispensation of understanding and judgement (on this notion of a 'talent', note again Kant's usage at G 4:393).

Such considerations tell against the standard view that mathematical sublimity is fully independent of dynamical sublimity. The two seem to need one another, and perhaps in somewhat different ways. For why, really, do we enjoy the assault on imagination in the mathematical sublime? Is it really enough to suppose that we are pleased to register the capacity of reason to conceive in pure thought what can never be met with in the senses? If what I have argued in this section is correct, then by Kant's lights this enjoyment is possible through a background commitment to distinctly moral ends. And if that is right, then what we appreciatively feel about our own rational capacity is that its own principle of freedom is the source of our own supersensible personhood: and we *care* to be persons, rather than mere things. All of this is simply more immediate, and in a sense thematic, in the dynamical sublime. Working from the other direction, the dynamical aspect of natural sublimity seems to need the mathematical *in concreto*: there is little reason to think that Kant is convinced that small poisonous beasts are sublime, à la Burke.[82] Kant seems nearer the mark when he suggests, through his litany of examples, that nature's might will impress us better when it also strikes us as immense.

With all this in mind, let me draw attention to two further details in CJ §27. Kant says that it *'belongs* to our vocation to estimate everything great that nature contains as an object of the senses for us as small in comparison with ideas of reason' (5:257).[83] It is part of our vocation to cultivate our cognitive capacities through exercise that accords with the regulative law of the theoretical reason; and we enjoy immense objects of nature as mathematically sublime inasmuch as they resonate with this calling. And later in CJ §27, Kant recapitulates how the immense object defeats the imagination in its efforts to comprehend the whole, inflicting a kind of 'violence' on it; he then adds that this 'very same violence ... is

---

[82] See §2.2.2, n24 and §3.3.2, n71.

[83] My emphasis. I have also altered the Cambridge translation (which has 'part of our vocation'): the German is *gehört zu unserer Bestimmung*. My rendering is more literal, but the Cambridge translation in fact captures Kant's point well.

judged as purposive **for the whole vocation** of the mind' (5:259). The immediate point of this remark is that the immense object figures as 'contrapurposive' for the imagination (as unamenable to its ends), but as 'purposive' for the human rational mind in its entirety. What might now strike us about this remark, however, is that Kant pointedly does not speak of what belongs to this vocation in this or that aspect of it. This 'whole vocation' must be understood as its cultivation according to its own rational principle, which ultimately calls for the cultivation of the will through the moral law. Therefore, while Kant does indeed distinguish mathematical and dynamical registers of our appreciation of natural sublimity, the whole package is underwritten by a background interest in essentially moral ends.

3.5 Conclusion

Kant undoubtedly walks a fine line. Moral cultivation can only figure as a background condition of the aesthetic judgement concerning natural sublimity: for this judgement cannot involve any determinate idea of the good if it is to be an *aesthetic* judgement in Kant's terms. But Kant also suggests that the enjoyment of nature's vastness and might *does something* to us: it produces a certain 'attunement of the mind [*Geistesstimmung*]' that is 'to be called sublime', rather than the natural object itself (CJ 5:250). What is this 'attunement'? It certainly cannot be virtue, or its distinctive temperament, since the judgement - once again - cannot directly involve any determinate idea of the good. And yet Kant insists this attunement is '*compatible with* that which the influence of determinate (practical) ideas on feeling would produce' (5:256, emphasis added). Indeed, this is how Kant explains our enjoyment of natural immensity in the first place: while the presentation of this immensity challenges our resources as *sensible* beings, it resonates with - indeed, even 'promotes' (recall 5:244) - our calling as essentially *rational* beings. These ideas are not precise; the picture is not sharp. But they can be reinforced if viewed from other angles as well. Any aesthetic judgement of reflection is disinterested, and contemplative: it does not rouse us to action, whether to pluck the beautiful flower, or to run from the mounting surf. Presumably it shouldn't rouse us to perform a noble deed – or do anything else besides. Natural beauty and sublimity alike seize us, hold us rapt. And yet in the case of the sublime, Kant contends, we only stand to be moved in the right way if we have prepared ourselves through the practice of *practical* judgement and the concomitant arousal of *moral* feeling. Only if we are ready to be moved by certain sorts of considerations are we in any condition to stand still, and enjoy the rude magnificence.[84]

4 Varieties of Sublime Feeling

Our exposition of the Analytic of the Sublime leaves us with some difficult questions. For the upshot was that a person's readiness to appreciate natural sublimity depends, on Kant's view, on a background commitment to essentially moral ends – a commitment, moreover, that can be more or less determinate and concretely action-guiding. This latter point, in fact, explains why Kant likens the aesthetic judgement of the sublime to 'a vibration, i.e., to a rapidly alternating repulsion from and attraction to one and the same object' (CJ §27 5:258). For he notes that the judgement is most like a vibration 'in its inception [*in ihrem Anfange*]', suggesting that it might become less so – and more stably governed by the attraction – as a person develops a more determinate and concretely action-guiding commitment to morally obligatory ends. Yet this only underscores the need for a reply to Herder. How can this background commitment to essentially moral ends inform our appreciation of natural sublimity without taking it over? Kant's answer turns on the idea that the

---

[84] Doran (2015:197) misunderstands my view in Merritt (2012): I do not claim that mathematical and dynamical sublimity align with a distinction between 'natural sublime' and 'moral sublime'. Rather, I take Kant's account of our appreciation of the sublimity of nature *as such* to require a background moral cultivation – which is, in effect, an attunement to the sublimity of the moral calling or human *Bestimmung*.

feeling by which we appreciate natural sublimity – admiration (*Bewunderung*) – is a close analogue of the moral feeling of respect (*Achtung*). My central aim in this section is to explain this analogy as clearly as Kant's texts permit. Once again, Kant's relation to prior tradition is significant, since many of his predecessors characterised sublime feeling as chiefly a kind of surprise, astonishment, or terror. Thus, it will be important to understand not only how Kant understands respect and admiration as distinct modes of sublime feeling, but also how and why he draws a line separating them from astonishment (*Verwunderung*) and other spurious contenders.

4.1 Respect

In the *Critique of Practical Reason* Kant provides an extended account of the moral-psychological phenomenon of respect – the feeling concomitant with our appreciation of moral requirement, or grasp of the moral law.[85] Respect is not itself a cognitive state: it is not the means by which we grasp the good, or understand what we objectively ought to do. Rather, Kant presents respect as the effect that the recognition of moral requirement has on *us* – specifically, on the feeling of embodied, imperfectly rational beings. This feeling is bivalent: repulsing in one aspect, attracting in another. This bivalence can be traced to our nature as both animal and rational, sensible and intelligible, beings. To understand Kant's account of respect, we will first need to elaborate his view of our moral condition as rational animals.

Kant takes the rational mind to be essentially reflective – a claim perhaps brought out best in his well-known version of the *cogito*: 'The *I think* must be *able* to accompany all of my representations' (CPR B131). Its implication, for specifically practical thought, is that we commit ourselves to maxims – i.e. principles expressing what we take as a reason for doing what – whenever we act intentionally at all: we so commit ourselves regardless of whether

---

[85] See also Kant's cursory sketch at G (4:401n).

we deliberately reflect upon what those principles are, and whether they are well-founded. The significance of this point is that it shows Kant to be committed to the idea that we are rational through and through, even when we act in the interest of sensible desire and 'inclination'. What is 'inclination' (*Neigung*)? Kant consistently defines it as 'habitual desire' (Anth 7:251, 265; MM 6:212; Rel 6:28). Patterns of pleasure and pain work themselves up into habitual desiderative dispositions, or inclinations. This is a given psychological fact about us, and not anything that we could coherently strive to free ourselves from. What this means, though, is that we are not immediately impelled towards the objects of our inclinations, but *take* them to be good and determine ourselves to attain them on that idea (CPrR 5:59-60). Moreover, if *good* is 'a necessary object of the faculty of desire ... in accordance with a principle of reason' (CPrR 5:58), then we are liable to comprehensively misvalue. The object of my inclination appeals to me given contingent facts about my physical constitution, including how it has been shaped by habit (which shaping is itself, most often, an expression and effect of intentional action). The object of my inclination is not a necessary object of desire for any rational being – it simply so happens to be an object of desire for me. We are liable to confuse what is properly a matter of preference for what is objectively good.

With this in mind, let us consider Kant's view of our moral condition. The second *Critique*'s Analytic sets out to argue that the constitutive principle of practical reason is the moral law (CPrR 5:19-57). The implication of this (quite controversial) claim is that anyone who has come into the use of her reason – and thus can think about what she ought to do – must have some tacit grasp of this principle, no matter how dim.[86] Yet as embodied rational beings with physical needs, it is a proper part of our nature – of

---

[86] This is the third predisposition to the good in the *Religion*, and the only one onto which no vices can be 'grafted' (6:27-8). The second is an interest to be honoured and respected by others: this is a natural expression of the self-consciousness of a rational being, but one from which all manner of 'vices of *culture*' can be grafted. And I am about to discuss the first.

our being what we properly ought to be – that we act to address these needs. In the *Religion,* Kant calls this the 'predisposition to animality in the human being', which he describes as a 'physical or merely *mechanical* self-love, i.e. a love for which reason is not required', and includes it within the 'original predisposition to the good in human nature' (6:26). Thus, he explicitly rejects the idea that the source of evil can coherently 'be placed, as is commonly done, in the sensuous nature of the human being, and in the natural inclinations originating from it' (Rel 6:34–5). This is an important, and easily misunderstood, point. The source of human badness ('radical evil') does not lie in our animal nature. In Kant's view it lies, rather, in the comprehensive misvaluing that is endemic to the imperfect practical rationality of the human being. Given the reflective nature of the rational mind, by default we take the object of inclination to be good, and endorse the claims of self-love as giving us reasons *before* all else (CPrR 5:74). When this commitment about value (the *goodness* of the objects of one's inclinations) is followed through to its natural conclusion, we come to take the claims of self-love to give us reasons *above* all else. The result is the '*self-conceit*' by which one arrogates one's own happiness as the necessary object of choice for any rational being (5:74).

Kant's account of respect starts with our propensity to validate the claims of self-love: 'we find our pathologically determinable self' – what we are as embodied rational beings – 'striving antecedently to make its claims primary and originally valid, just as if it constituted our entire self' (CPrR 5:74). But by setting ends freely and acting on them, we take ourselves to be persons rather than mere things; and in so doing, we tacitly grasp the principle of our personality, the moral law. When a person has an active thought about moral requirement, or recognises its standard manifest in another's conduct or character, the result '*strikes down* self-conceit, that is humiliates it' (5:73; also 5:74). This involves a comparison – and thus, by Kant's lights, a reflective rational activity (Rel 6:27) – between two claims about value. But the determination of value issued by the principle of self-love can only be annihilated by the good grasped through the moral law: 'Hence the moral law unavoidably humiliates every human being when he compares it with the sensible propensity of his nature' (CPrR 5:74). Yet we are talking about a single human being who, at least tacitly, grasps that the annihilating principle issues from his own rational nature. And thus 'the effect which on the one side is merely *negative*' – and is experienced as painful repulsion – 'on the other side . . . is *positive*' (5:75), at least inasmuch as one recognises that one is properly a person, not a thing, and thus ought to be governed by the moral law, this principle of personality.

That final qualification is important for appreciating the phenomenological range of the feeling of respect.[87] Although Kant takes the absence of any capacity for moral feeling to be something like monstrous (MM-DV 6:399–400),[88] so that by his lights the feeling of respect is concomitant with the appreciation of moral requirement in any normal human being, it is nevertheless possible not to feel respect with any appreciable duration. For the humiliation of the claims of self-love is unpleasant, and we naturally move to avoid pain: we might find ways of redirecting our attention, or redescribing the situation we find ourselves in, so that we are no longer *struck* in this way.[89] But if one does have some commitment to one's moral personality, then one cannot help but to feel respect with one's recognition of moral requirement (or its exemplar), and feel it with some (however minimal) duration.

---

[87] At one point Kant gives the impression that the feeling of respect arises when the claims of morality are experienced as having a greater weight *relative to* the claims of self-love (CPrR 5:76). But by Kant's own lights the comparison at issue should strictly speaking be an *annihilating* one, as he indicates in his initial gloss of humiliation (5:74) – on this see also Reath (1989:289n13 and 296). Perhaps Kant's point is that the comparison is annihilating only in the fully virtuous, where the moral law *silences* any claim about objective value issued by self-love. Since Kant maintains that the source of such claims is part of human nature, and virtue involves no transcendence of the human condition (CPrR 5:84–6), the 'silencing' metaphor from McDowell (1979) seems apt here.

[88] Or perhaps a psychopathology; see Kennett (2015).

[89] Kant makes this point particularly with regards to esteem respect (CPrR 5:77), which we will consider in the next section.

4.2 *Admiration and Respect As Feelings of the Sublime*

Having considered Kant's account of respect in the second *Critique*, we now need to examine its bearing on the third *Critique*'s Analytic of the Sublime. Recall Kant's account of how our enjoyment of sublimity differs from our enjoyment of beauty: the pleasure involved 'arises only indirectly, being generated, namely, by the feeling of a momentary inhibition of the vital powers and the immediately following and all the more powerful outpouring of them' (CJ 5:245). An inhibiting stress upon powers of one sort invigorates the expression of powers of another sort. Since the object that occasions this response is both repulsive and attractive, 'the satisfaction in the sublime does not so much contain positive pleasure as it does *admiration or respect* [*Bewunderung oder Achtung*], i.e., it deserves to be called *negative pleasure*' (5:245; my emphasis). This might be read as an appositive disjunction,[90] were it not for the clear distinction that Kant draws between admiration and respect in the second *Critique*:

> *Respect* is always directed only to persons, never to things. The latter can awaken in us *inclination* and even *love* if they are animals (e.g., horses, dogs, and so forth), or also *fear*, like the sea, a volcano, a beast of prey, but never *respect*. Something that comes nearer to this feeling is *admiration* [*Bewunderung*], and this as an affect, amazement [*Erstaunen*], can be directed to things also, for example, lofty mountains, the magnitude, number, and distance of the heavenly bodies, the strength and swiftness of many animals, and so forth. But none of this is respect. (CPrR 5:76)[91]

Here Kant points to many of the stock examples of natural sublimity, and explicitly denies that the appropriate feeling could be respect. Instead, he names *admiration* and *amazement* as the

---

[90] As Doran (2015:197) reads it, assuming that Kant's remark here is restricted to the appreciation of *natural* sublimity; but Kant nowhere says it is.

[91] When Kant says that our feeling for natural sublimity is 'a kind of respect' (CJ 5:249), on the basis of this passage we can only take him to mean *something like* respect for the moral law, but not, of course, that very feeling itself.

feelings that takes such things as their proper objects. On the basis of the above we should rule out the idea that respect could be the feeling by which we appreciate natural sublimity.

My aim in this subsection is to explain Kant's view of the difference between admiration and respect, while accounting for his view of each as feelings for the sublime. They must be deeply enough alike – or closely enough 'analogous' to one another (see CPrR 5:78) – to underwrite Kant's own way of developing the received idea that sublimity is absolute greatness. At the same time, we need to see whether Kant's account of their relation leaves him with a satisfying reply to Herder-style objections:[92] how can our moral appreciation of absolute value inform the aesthetic appreciation of natural sublimity without taking it over?

We might be puzzled by Kant's remark that respect can only be directed to persons, not things – since, after all, his account first concerns respect for *the moral law*: while the moral law is not a 'thing', it is not obviously a person, either. But the moral law is the principle of personality, and so Kant treats respect for the moral law as the genus under which distinct species of respect for particular persons – recognition respect and esteem respect – can be determined. (Of these, we will concern ourselves only with esteem respect.[93]) Kant presents esteem respect through a memorable vignette of finding himself *moved* by the example that a 'common humble man' sets for him. We are invited to imagine a person of extremely modest means who (say) gives generously to others – he gives more, and more gladly, than Kant himself ever does. Respect is wrung from him: '*my spirit bows*, whether I want it or whether I do not and

---

[92] See §3.1.

[93] See G (4:401n): 'The *object* of respect is ... simply the [moral] *law* ... Any respect for a person is properly only respect for the law (of righteousness [*Rechtschaffenheit*] and so forth) of which he gives us an example.' Recognition respect doesn't figure in this remark at all, since it is owed to vicious scoundrels just as it is owed to the righteous (MM-DV 6:462–3) – and indeed only becomes a focus of Kant's ethics in this later work, though it is implicit in the *Groundwork* account of human dignity. See Darwall (1977 and 2008) on the distinction between esteem respect and recognition respect.

hold my head ever so high, that he may not overlook my superior position' (CPrR 5:77).

In the wake of this vignette, Kant points out that a display of remarkable talent and skill is often an occasion to feel *admiration* – but not, at least in most instances, *respect* (CPrR 5:78). This discussion is complicated, because he first denies that a person's talents are properly an occasion even for admiration at all, at least if they are given endowments. I have a friend who has 360-degree turnout in his feet: i.e. he can stand with his feet facing the opposite direction as the front of his body. I find this astonishing, but not admirable.[94] But a person's cultivated talents, or skills, can properly be admired – at least if they strike one as something great, and at least somewhat out of the ordinary. Is the good character of the 'common humble man' from the earlier vignette properly *admired* then? Kant denies this:

> This respect ... which we show to a person (strictly speaking to the law that his example holds before us) is not mere admiration, as is also confirmed by this: that when the common run of admirers believes it has somehow learned the badness of character of such a man (such as Voltaire) it gives up all respect for him, whereas a true scholar still feels it at least with regard to his talents, because he is himself engaged in a business and a calling that make imitation of such a man to some extent law for him.   (CPrR 5:78)

Kant's example of the layperson's admiration for a public intellectual such as Voltaire is similar to my admiration for an Olympic gymnast such as Simone Biles: it is her skill I admire. I do not have any remotely determinate practical understanding of what it would be to run through such a tumbling sequence, or to turn a backflip on a balance beam. All of that is entirely off the radar of my agential possibilities, or interests. I do not, at least as far as sport goes, share her ends. As a result, her shining example does not compel me to do anything. Admiration is not exhortative. But *respect* is. For the scholar who has somehow learned, along with everyone else, that

---

[94] We will return to the distinction between astonishment and admiration in §4.3.

Voltaire is a *bad human being* (full stop) may still respect him as a *good scholar*: Voltaire's example (as a scholar) provides a model for his efforts (as a scholar).[95] Thus, Kant suggests that I can respect another for her skills if I share the discretionary end that governs the skill. If I do not share this end, then I can only *admire* her skill, and only then if it strikes me as something great – worth having, and at least somewhat outside of the ordinary run of things. But I stand to respect another human being as a good *person* only inasmuch as I share the non-discretionary, morally obligatory, end of cultivating good character in myself.[96]

From this we can see why admiration might suitably figure as the feeling for natural sublimity. For we enjoy natural sublimity through an aesthetic judgement of reflection, and such judgements are *contemplative*:[97] they do not directly exhort us to action. As Brady (2013:81) suggests, this allows us to enjoy nature for its own sake, independently of our own ends.[98] Moreover, Kant points to the pedagogical dangers of arousing mere *admiration* for ostensible figures of virtue; a moral education needs, rather, to arouse genuine respect in order to help someone develop good character.[99] Thus, the non-exhortative character of admiration shows it to be a more suitable candidate for the feeling for natural sublimity than respect.

---

[95] At least if these can be neatly separated. Kant's Voltaire example makes me think of the struggle that philosophers face, and should face, over Heidegger's Nazism: can we respect him *as a philosopher*, if we cannot respect him as a good human being?

[96] This paragraph rehearses points from Merritt (2012 and 2017). However, I wonder if admiration *can* be exhortative; at any rate, admiration strikes me as being the appropriate attitude to someone with whom you share a discretionary end in some endeavour but yet is of vastly greater skill (e.g., my taekwondo teacher who is an 9th-dan black belt Grand Master). I *admire* his skill because it lies beyond what I can make full practical sense of, but I nevertheless arguably aspire to his example.

[97] Because the liking involved is 'disinterested'; see §3.

[98] She marshals this point as an avenue of reply to Herder-style objections (see §3.1).

[99] See CPrR Doctrine of Method, which I discuss in Merritt (2011); and note Kant's usage, 'admired but not on that account sought', at CPrR (5:160).

Finally, one further difference between the moral feeling of respect and the feeling for natural sublimity should be noted. At the outset of this section, I quoted Kant's presentation of the latter as a 'negative pleasure' that arises 'indirectly' from some initial assault on our cognitive powers. We might read this simply as a gloss of its bivalence, that some painful aversion is part of the story about how we come to enjoy sublimity. But it reveals, I think, somewhat more than this. For Kant presents respect for the moral law as similarly indirect, and bivalent. However, he also says that 'respect for the moral law must be regarded as also a *positive though indirect* effect of the moral law on feeling insofar as the law weakens the hindering influence of the inclinations by humiliating self-conceit' (CPrR 5:79; my emphasis). We stand to take a kind of pleasure in this humiliation because, but only inasmuch as, we care to make ourselves genuinely good; and we do so on the grounds that 'whatever diminishes the hindrances to an activity is a furthering of the activity itself' (5:79). We take an *interested* pleasure in this, through a determinate practical commitment to a conception of the good. Kant needs to avoid all of this in his account of our appreciation of natural sublimity. He must accordingly avoid any suggestion that we enjoy natural sublimity for any contribution it might make to the formation of good character. So he presents this enjoyment as indirect *and negative* pleasure.

But this seems stipulative, a mere form of words designed to block any implication of an interested liking. Kant wants to avoid the Burkean implications of a 'merely negative pleasure': a liking that is *simply* to be understood as a release from stress or pain. Intuitively, the richness of our experiences of natural sublimity – that we linger, and are held rapt – requires that we are actively pulled *towards* something. Otherwise we just enjoy it for the thrill. Kant wants to suggest that our interest in morality accounts for the richness, and direction, of our enjoyment of natural sublimity; but he also wants to keep any determinate moral commitments running in the background, making the aesthetic judgement possible, but not taking part in it as such.

How does Kant presume to pull this off? If there is an answer, it lies in understanding how admiration is like respect in having the expression of rational agency as its proper object. But this very point strains its anointed role as the feeling of natural sublimity. Indeed, there are two reasons why admiration should seem a poor candidate for the feeling for natural sublimity. First, in the context where Kant explains what admiration is, he takes its proper object to be skills and other expressions of rational agency. What does it then mean to speak of admiring a swelling surf and so on? Second, admiration does not seem to have the characteristic bivalence that Kant's account of natural sublimity requires. What exactly is the repelling side of my admiration for Simone Biles's gymnastic skill? Since I do not care to be a gymnast myself, we can hardly chalk it up to envy. To answer these questions, it will help to consider how Kant's contemporary, Moses Mendelssohn, distinguished admiration (*Bewunderung*) from astonishment (*Verwunderung*), and developed an account of the former as a proper feeling of the sublime. As we will see, Kant endorses Mendelssohn's view that admiration, not astonishment, should be admitted as a proper feeling for the sublime. But he cannot endorse Mendelssohn's resulting account – and seeing why will bring into sharper relief the philosophical pressures giving shape to Kant's own account of the sublime.

4.3   Lessons from Mendelssohn

Why *does* Kant suggest that admiration is the feeling paradigmatically involved in our appreciation of natural sublimity? The answer, at least in part, lies in Kant's endorsement of a critical move that Moses Mendelssohn makes against the idea that the proper feeling of the sublime could be anything like astonishment, terror, or pity. Beiser (2009:208, 219) traces the source of this move to a series of letters that Mendelssohn wrote to G. E. Lessing, contesting that admiration (not pity) is the proper emotion of tragedy – a point that Mendelssohn eventually extends to the sublime more generally in the 1761 *Philosophical Writings*, where he has Abbé Dubos and Edmund Burke in his sights as well.[100] There Mendelssohn takes aim against theories that understand our enjoyment of the sublime as a kind of thrill, an exercise that relieves boredom, or a respite from strain. For all such theories trace our enjoyment of sublimity to a weakness or *incapacity* of mind; but sublimity must arouse positive powers 'of knowing and desiring' in a way that stands to *elevate* or perfect them.[101] Mendelssohn eventually names admiration (*Bewunderung*) as the feeling that fits the bill,[102] and says that the paradigmatic object of admiration is not any bodily or physical perfection, but rather 'perfections of spirit ... and generally all great qualities of a spirit that take us by surprise and sweep up our soul with them, elevating it, as it were, above itself' (1997:198 [1929: I.461]).

In this context, Mendelssohn distinguishes admiration (*Bewunderung*) from astonishment (*Verwunderung*): both have a sense of shock at what is unexpected, or stands out from the normal run of things; but admiration has an evaluative component – its object is something exceptionally and '*unexpectedly good*' (1997:198n [1929:I.461n]). Mendelssohn thus distinguishes astonishment and admiration as genus and species, which yields an account of admiration's bivalence. The negative aspect of admiration can be attributed to the 'pain' of incomprehension that belongs to it as a species of astonishment; the positive aspect

---

[100] See Mendelssohn (1997:71 and 146–7 [1929: I.304 and 400–1]) on Abbé Dubos and Edmund Burke, respectively.

[101] See Mendelssohn's 'Rhapsody' in his *Philosophical Writings* (1997:134 and 136 [1929:I.386 and 389]). See also the similar point that Mendelssohn makes in the earlier 'Dialogues on Sentiments' about our enjoyment of beauty (1997:19, 23–4 [1929: I.248, 252]), bearing in mind that in the German rationalist tradition sublimity is an aspect of beauty rather than essentially distinct from it (as noted in §2.3).

[102] See Mendelssohn (1997:195 [1929:I.458]). For purposes of consistency, I am not following Dahlstrom in rendering *Bewunderung* with 'awe', but with 'admiration' (as it has been translated from Kant's texts). Given Mendelssohn's somewhat high-flown account of *Bewunderung*, Dahlstrom's rendering makes some sense; but Dahlstrom also sometimes reverts to 'awe and admiration' to render the single word *Bewunderung*, which threatens to confuse an English reader's sense of the German text.

stems from the appreciation of the extraordinary thing as *good*. Simone Biles's skill assaults my sense of what is possible in the order of things – this is the disagreeable aspect – but *what* I admire is a cultivated human excellence that itself stretches my view of the possibilities of human action – and that is agreeable. Admiration is thus shown to be suitably bivalent, and in such a way that indicates how it might be informed by practical reason, but without directly engaging it: it is, once again, a contemplative, not an exhortative, appreciation of her skill.

In many respects, Kant follows suit. In his *Anthropology*, he explains astonishment (*Verwunderung*)[103] as a 'confusion' occasioned by something unexpected, something that 'at first impedes the natural play of thought' – which makes it partly unpleasant, except that the surprise 'later . . . promotes the influx of thought to the unexpected representation all the more and thus becomes an agreeable excitement of feeling' (Anth 7:261). Thus, astonishment appears to have a mixed nature, which prima facie might qualify it as a feeling of the sublime. The painful aspect of astonishment stems from an assault on our cognitive capacities – we encounter something so surprising that we cannot quite fit it into our sense of the normal order of things – and the pleasurable aspect stems from the stimulation this puzzlement gives to those same cognitive capacities.[104] And while Kant does seem to allow that 'an

---

[103] Here I am not following Louden, who renders *Verwunderung* as 'surprise' in this passage of the Cambridge Edition.

[104] One difficulty of Kant's account of astonishment (*Verwunderung*) is his presentation of it as an *affect* (see CPrR 5:272 and Anth 7:261), for he also says that astonishment 'already contains reflection in itself' (Anth 7:255) – which is not compatible with his view that affect momentarily suspends all reflection, or powers of self-conscious thought (see 5:272n, Anth 7:254; MM-DV 6:407–8). Perhaps the tension among Kant's claims can be lessened if we allow that astonishment cannot be pure, unadulterated affect – but affect in only one moment, or aspect. Then Kant's point about astonishment's 'containing reflection' might be interpreted as follows. The astonishing thing stands out against the background of one's grip on the general order of things (it stands out as *not fitting in*); but for that to register, one must tacitly compare it against an idea of the whole, and in this sense it 'contains reflection'. But when the astonishment is so great that one is no longer sure if one is dreaming or

astonishment bordering on terror' can help involve a person's imagination in a 'sublime' landscape (CJ 5:269), he otherwise suggests that the overall feeling for this sublimity must be some kind of admiration if one is to be compelled in any sustained way (CJ 5:272). Thus, he rejects pure astonishment as a feeling of the sublime, inasmuch as the incomprehension can be a deterrent to 'feeling our own greatness and power'; and again suggests that admiration better fits the bill of sublime feeling, as a kind of 'judgment in which we do not grow weary of being astonished' (Anth 7:243; see also CJ 5:365) – we do not grow weary, presumably, because it offers some positive satisfaction of our rational capacity.

Yet while Kant accepts the broad outlines of Mendelssohn's distinction between admiration and astonishment, and while he endorses Mendelssohn's critical point against theorists such as Dubos and Burke, he cannot endorse Mendelssohn's positive account of admiration as the feeling of the sublime. To see why, we will need to take a closer look at the distinct ways in which Mendelssohn and Kant draw from Stoic sources in their respective theories of the sublime, which is our topic for the next section.

5   Starry Heavens: Stoic Sources of the Kantian Sublime

My aim in this concluding section is to trace some of the Stoic sources of Kant's account of the sublime: this should leave us with a sharper view of the philosophical pressures that ultimately give Kant's account of the sublime its distinctive shape. I will principally examine the matter of this Stoic influence through Kant's engagement with Moses Mendelssohn's theory of the sublime – and especially in their respective presentations of what may well be

perceiving an objective independent world, then one loses the sort of self-conscious grip on one's own thought that *is* characteristic of affect (Anth 7:261). Thus, Kant's overarching point might be that astonishment tends towards affect. But if this astonishment 'promotes the influx of thought' (7:261), it cannot be *pure* affect; it can only have an aspect of affect just inasmuch as the astonishing thing seems to be incomprehensible, thereby inhibiting – at least very briefly – the capacity for self-conscious thought.

the ultimate stock example of the sublime: the starry night sky.[105] The sublimity of the heavens is a Stoic trope in the letters of Seneca, and Kant's engagement with Mendelssohn turns on what to accept and reject of the Stoic legacy on the sublime, with a particular eye to Seneca. I begin, though, with Kant's endorsement of *apathy* as 'an entirely correct and sublime moral principle of the Stoic school' (Anth 7:253).

5.1 Apathy and Enthusiasm

In §3.3.2, we identified a turning point in Kant's account of the dynamical sublime: the sensible presentation of nature's might is fearful, since it suggests a power that could obliterate one's existence and any measure of wellbeing; and yet we stand to enjoy it inasmuch as we recognise some other standard of value, and thus that something in us is unthreatened by such power (5:263; quoted in §3.3.2). Here Kant invokes a familiar Stoic idea of facing one's material circumstances with calm equanimity, imbued with a standing readiness to regard worldly goods – and even health and life itself – as 'small' or 'trivial' (*klein*) when their attainment or preservation comes into contest with what morality requires (CJ 5:262). It is worth pointing out that the same characteristically Stoic idea is invoked by Longinus in a prominent place in his essay on the sublime – though not, as we will see, with any thoroughgoing commitment to Stoicism.

Longinus's treatise on the sublime is pragmatic: it is largely concerned with how literary technique can arouse sublimity of mind, and allow us to 'develop our natures to some degree of grandeur' (*On the Sublime* 1.1 [1995:160–1]). He points to five

---

[105] I cannot here trace the various ways in which the 'starry heavens' example is put to use across the history of writing on the sublime; but for some examples from Kant's Anglophone predecessors, see: Joseph Addison, *Spectator* no. 412 (Bond 1965 [v.3]:540), John Baillie in Ashfield and de Bolla (1996:88), Edmund Burke *Enquiry* II.xiii (1990:71), James Beattie in Ashfield and de Bolla (1996:181), Hugh Blair in Ashfield and de Bolla (1996:213), and Thomas Reid *Essays* VIII.iii (1969:772).

main 'sources' of the sublime – *productive* sources (πηγαί, literally 'springs'), not sources in the sense of the governing principles of a theory or system (ἀρχαί). Right before he does so, he invokes, as a piece of common wisdom, the characteristically Stoic idea at issue:

> We must realise ... that as in our everyday life nothing is really great which it is a mark of greatness to despise, I mean, for instance, wealth, honour, reputation, sovereignty, and all the other things which possess a very grand exterior, nor would a wise man think things supremely good, contempt for which is itself eminently good – certainly men feel less admiration for those who have these things than for those who could have them but are big enough to slight them – well, so it is with the lofty style in poetry and prose.
>
> (*On the Sublime* 7.1 [1995:178–9])

Longinus's local point is that a writer of truly 'sublime' poetry and prose eschews the dazzling literary moves that she might perfectly well know how to execute; and this is something like the sage who slights the wealth and power that may be in his power to claim from a principled concern to cultivate what is truly good. Virtue is indeed the *sole* good for the Stoic.[106] So, this at first looks like a mere analogy, with limited implications for Longinus's substantive view. However, he immediately thereafter claims that sublime writing should be universally uplifting, pleasing 'all people at all times' (7.4 [180–1]), implying that such writing should draw us towards what is objectively good – like the Stoic's idea of virtue. Longinus next turns to the 'first and most powerful' source of the sublime, which he names as 'the power to form grand conceptions' (8.1 [180–1]). Sublimity comes chiefly from the capacity to have thoughts of the right sort, about suitably great things. But it also, Longinus contends, comes from 'violent and enthusiastic emotion [τὸ σφοδρὸν καὶ ἐνθουσιαστικὸν πάθος]' (8.1 [180–1]). These are the two natural or congenital sources of the sublime, which Longinus

---

[106] This is a fundamental tenet of Stoic ethics: see, e.g., Diogenes Laertius in Long and Sedley (1987) 58A; or Seneca *Letters* 76.6–16 and 85.20 (Seneca 2015:240–1 and 291).

distinguishes from the remaining three that lie in technical aspects of writing.

Kant rejects the Longinian idea of 'violent and enthusiastic emotion' as a proper source of the sublime in the third *Critique*.[107] To be precise, Kant does not deny that the spirit can soar through the power of emotion: he calls this '**enthusiasm [*Enthusiasmus*]**', which he defines as 'the idea of the good *with affect*' (CJ 5:272; my italics). Now, it is generally true that through the force of violent emotion we might find ourselves doing things we wouldn't ordinarily have it in ourselves to do;[108] enthusiasm is the species of this phenomenon where the driving emotion is positively charged or *uplifting* (as anger, say, is not) and thereby arouses us to what appears to be *good*. So Kant acknowledges, in a backhanded way, that enthusiasm 'seems to be sublime [*scheint erhaben*]' (5:272), because through it one's spirit seems to soar. And maybe, in some sense, it does – but not in any salutary way. For affect, Kant explains, is overwhelming feeling that momentarily suspends one's capacity for self-conscious thought.[109] Affect seizes a person's (typically tacit) grip on herself as the source of a point of view on how things are and what is worth doing. But how then can someone aroused by affect so much as entertain an idea of an action as good? The uplifted state of mind can only be a result of something's *working on* you, *driving* you in ways that you are not (for the duration of affect) in any position to understand, or reflectively assess. Any idea of the good involved can only be vague and

---

[107] Although Longinus was studied almost universally by theorists of the sublime in the eighteenth century (including Mendelssohn), Kant was very likely not thinking of Longinus directly in this passage – but rather, as I will suggest, Mendelssohn. See also Doran (2015:176).

[108] As we noted in §2.3, examining Baumgarten's quotation of Seneca on anger. Kant alludes in this passage to the Stoic argument against the idea that we need powerful emotion to accomplish great things.

[109] This emerges in Kant's distinction between affect and passion – a very interesting story in its own right, but one that needs to be bracketed for present purposes. See CJ (5:272n), as well as MM-DV (6:407–8) and Anth (7:252). I discuss Kant's distinction between affect and passion at some length in Merritt (2018).

indistinct, and something that figures inasmuch as we are subject to external influence and manipulation – politically, pedagogically, religiously, and so on. So when Kant concludes that 'enthusiasm is aesthetically sublime' (5:272), he marks it off from any sublimity that could be the expression of self-determined human reason.[110]

This point has not been well understood by commentators, presumably because Kant analyses our appreciation of natural sublimity under the heading of the '*aesthetic* judgment of reflection', which might give the impression that he has been talking about the 'aesthetically sublime' all along. But (as we saw in §3.2) the aesthetic judgement of *reflection* is grounded in a certain satisfaction of our cognitive powers – and, in the case of the sublime, a satisfaction of reason with regard to its practical capacity. So the type of 'uplifted' frame of mind that Kant analyses at length in the Analytic of the Sublime cannot be one that is made possible through affect, or 'aesthetically'. Moreover, Kant underscores his rejection of enthusiasm with his immediately ensuing endorsement of the Stoic duty of apathy: we ought to make ourselves less susceptible to such overwhelming feeling. Indeed, in the *Metaphysics of Morals*, Kant presents apathy as a *necessary* condition of virtue (6:408–9): it is required to overcome the endemic human liability to misvalue.[111] It 'seems strange', Kant acknowledges, but 'even **affectlessness** (*apatheia* ...) in a mind that emphatically pursues its own inalterable principles is sublime, and indeed in a far superior way, because it also has the satisfaction of pure reason on its side' (CJ 5:272). It *seems strange* because sublimity is inescapably, for Kant and many others, an expression of feeling and temperament. But the source and nature of the feeling makes all the difference; and for Kant, as I've argued,

---

[110] Cf. Clewis (2009) for a more sanguine view of enthusiasm in Kant's account of the sublime.

[111] I discussed Kant's account of this liability in §4.1. But everything turns on the precise sense in which we can, in principle, overcome this liability. We cannot overcome it by transcending human nature, so that we are no longer subject to non-moral incentives on action: this, Kant thinks, is the risk that Stoic ethics courts, as it holds up its model of the sage (CPrR 5:127n).

sublimity is essentially connected to the rationally grounded feeling of respect.

The immediate target of Kant's discussion of enthusiasm and apathy appears to be Moses Mendelssohn's discussion of humility and human nature in his *Philosophical Writings*. Mendelssohn argues that moral humility is properly directed at oneself, not the whole human race: one must, in other words, regard one's own moral cultivation in a sceptical light, while remaining firmly committed to the essential goodness of human beings – that is, our in-principle capacity to make ourselves genuinely virtuous. Should we adopt a view of human nature that invites us to suppose that genuine goodness lies beyond our ken, then moral depravity will inevitably result. Thus, Mendelssohn contends, we 'must become acquainted with the true dignity of the human being and consider the sublimity of the human being's ethical nature in the proper light' (1997:165 [1929:I.420]). *The proper light* is with humility: looking up to this standard, and measuring oneself against it. One is not measuring oneself against anything other than one's own essential nature as a human being, a rational animal. So far, so good. Kant, at any rate, makes much the same point about humility in the third *Critique*: 'Even humility . . . is a sublime state of mind, that of voluntarily subjecting oneself to the pain of self-reproach in order gradually to eliminate the causes of it' (5:264). Humility is a glad commitment to an ideal from which one should always appear to fall short. The bivalence of this, and thus its sublimity, should be familiar to us by now. But Mendelssohn develops this idea in ways that Kant cannot endorse:

> One should learn to consider every human action in connection with the ever-present lawgiver of nature and in relation to eternity. One should get used to having these considerations before one's eyes in every act that one performs. If one does this a wholesome enthusiasm [*heilsamer Enthusiasmus*] for virtue will be awakened in us, and each reason motivating us to be virtuous will attain an ethical majesty through which its influence and its effectiveness on the will is strengthened. (Mendelssohn 1997:16 [1929:I.421])

While Kant agrees with Mendelssohn that we should not consider our own individual failings as the inevitable expression of endemic human weakness, he lodges a pointed critique of Mendelssohn's view of what it is to cultivate ourselves, as rational beings, into a state of moral *health*. Mendelssohn suggests here that we ought to consider our every action in relation to a divine lawgiver. But on what epistemic grounds do we take this comparison to be intelligible? On what basis can we take ourselves to be so much as able to have a determinate thought of the place of any human action 'in relation to eternity'? Though we can look up to an ideal of character, to the perfection of virtue, its goodness must in principle be fully appreciable from where we stand. For Kant, in other words, a 'wholesome enthusiasm for virtue' is a contradiction in terms.[112]

5.2 Starry Heavens

Kant's argument against enthusiasm is closely connected to his famous 'starry heavens' passage that concludes the second *Critique* – a passage that, as I will suggest, is best understood as a tussle with Mendelssohn over what to accept and reject from the Stoic philosophical legacy, at least as regards a modern theory of the sublime. Since the sublimity of the starry night sky was a particular speciality of the Roman Stoic, Seneca, I will begin with the evidence that gives us reason to suppose that Seneca is indeed their shared and particular point of reference.[113]

Seneca compares the mind of the virtuous person – the Stoic sage – with the starry night sky several times in his letters to his younger friend, Lucilius, on the therapeutic power of Stoic philosophy. The mind of the sage and the starry heavens are alike

---

[112] Ultimately, Kant's point is that if we allow ourselves to be impelled by feeling to do 'good' on terms that we do not genuinely understand – if we allow ourselves to be morally uplifted through vehement feeling, and welcome *Enthusiasmus* – then we expose ourselves to 'enthusiasm' of a much more dangerous sort: *Schwärmerei*. I will return to this in §5.2.

[113] See also Santokzi (2012:225–7) on the Senecan sources of Kant's 'starry heavens' passage.

'eternally serene' (*Letters* 59.16 [2015:175]). What is the basis of this serenity? The sage is no longer subject to the chronic misvaluing that afflicts the ordinary human being. Here a brief note on the Stoic duty of apathy, and the 'eupathic' ideal of the virtuous person, is necessary. The Stoics call the basic elements of mental content 'impressions', which they distinguish as rational or non-rational, depending on whether they are had by rational or non-rational animals. Rational impressions are correlated with proposition-like items that the Stoics call *axiōmata*. Human adults have *rational* impressions, which means that the propositional content bound up in the impression is subject to assent or rejection. A rational impression is then a suggestion about how things are; and the propositional content may be evaluative, and thus involve ideas of what it is fitting to do. Impressions of this sort are 'impulsive'[114] – a way of being struck by how things are that impels one to act. Typically, this assent is a matter of acquiescence – tacit reliance on the proposition for thought and action. Emotions (*pathē*) are a species of rational impulse, and thus involve opinion or judgement about good and bad. But on the Stoic view, these judgements are all false. A person who is subject to *pathē* – more or less everyone – regularly and comprehensively misvalues, takes what is at best to be valued for its positive planning value for what is genuinely good, and takes what is at best to be avoided for its negative planning value for what is genuinely bad.[115] A sage is *apathēs* – no longer subject to *pathē* – and therefore no longer makes false judgements about value. Yet there is nevertheless a felt quality of consciousness – a *temperament* – concomitant with correct valuing, one constituted by the *eupatheiai*, centrally joy. And Seneca recommends the Stoic path on this basis: 'Thus you have reason to desire wisdom if wisdom is always accompanied by joy. But this joy has only one source: a consciousness of the virtues' (*Letters* 59.16 [2015:175]) – it is the concomitant expression, in

---

[114] φαντασία ὁρμητική: Stobaeus in Long and Sedley (1987) 53Q.
[115] I've drawn throughout this paragraph on Brennan (2003), and borrow the phrase 'positive planning value' from him (2003:271).

feeling, of one's recognition of the one true good: virtue. Such joy, in one who has attained virtue, can only be an abiding temperament: it 'has no intermission and no end' (59.18 [2015:176]).[116]

The heavens are a natural wonder that we cannot touch: we see them from some unfathomable remove. What follows, then, for the attainability of virtue? Seneca mentions with approval an earlier Roman philosopher who was not an avowed Stoic,[117] for demonstrating 'the magnitude of true happiness' without robbing you of 'your hope of achieving it' (64.5 [2005:184]):

> The same attitude is inspired by virtue itself, namely that you admire [*admireris*] it and yet hope to achieve it. For me, at least, the very thought of wisdom absorbs much of my time. I am no less astonished [*obstupefactus*] when I gaze at it than I am sometimes by the heavens themselves, which I often see as if for the first time.
> (Letters 64.6 [2005:184])[118]

Gazing at the heavens is a physical model of the proper orientation of a human mind to a perfection that lies at an unfathomable – but not, for that, uncrossable – remove. 'Just as our bodily posture is erect, with its gaze towards the heavens, so our mind can stretch forth as far as it wishes, having been formed by the very nature of the world to want things on the divine scale' (92.30 [2015:347]). We do not, apparently, require divine assistance to make the crossing: the human mind's only route there is distinctly 'its own' (92.30 [2015:347]). Although Seneca does not elaborate here, his point can only be that we make this progress solely by exercising distinctively human resources of judgement to correct, and ultimately overcome, our endemic liability to misvalue.

---

[116] See also Seneca, *Constantia* 9.3 (2014:158); and Graver (2016) for an excellent study of Senecan joy.

[117] 'Quintus Sextius the Elder – a great man ... and a Stoic, even if he denies it' (2015:183).

[118] An anonymous reader asks whether Seneca's appeal to admiration (and astonishment) rather than respect tells against my claims about his influence. I think it is unreasonable to expect a claim of Seneca's influence to rest on his adhering to conceptual distinctions that were arguably only made fully explicit, and at any rate characteristically developed, by Kant.

Kant, we should now be able to see, endorses much of this. And with Seneca, he recognises that virtue can only be acquired from a default starting point of error, faultiness, or sin: 'All of us have been taken over already, and to learn virtue is to unlearn one's faults' (*Letters* 50.7 [2015:146]). The crucial difference is that, for Kant, virtue cannot be conceived as a kind of security against the endemic human tendency to misvalue. Indeed, his main complaint against the Stoic tradition is chiefly the assumption that the sage has *transcended* human nature (CPrR 5:127 n). But Seneca, at least, is somewhat ambivalent on this very point. For he says in *Consolation to Helvia* 8.5 that 'there is always the same distance between all things divine and all things human' (Seneca 2014:56) – perhaps suggesting that no matter how wise any human being may be, she is for that no closer to godhood. Yet in *Constantia* 15.2, Seneca's remark on the sage invites Kant's complaint: 'his virtue locates him in another part of the universe: he has nothing in common with you' (Seneca 2014:164) – he is out there in some 'beyond', with the gods. Incidentally, Vogt reports that the early Stoics, at least, took some of the gods to be *planets* (2008:13) – which, if true,[119] might cast Seneca's 'starry heavens' passages in a new light. To look out at the starry night sky is, then, quite literally to behold perfectly rational beings. Kant may have had this in mind when he wrote, in the margin of his own published copy of his 1764 *Observations on the Feeling of the Beautiful and Sublime*: 'We can see other worlds in the distance, but gravity forces us to remain on the earth; we can see other perfections in spirits above us, but our nature forces us to remain human beings' (20:153).[120] It's an elegant riposte to the Senecan trope of the starry heavens.

That said, Seneca's striking way of holding, in one and the same breath, the loftiness of the heavens alongside the loftiness of the sage left its mark on both Mendelssohn and Kant.[121] The starry

---

[119] Unfortunately she does not cite the textual basis for this claim.

[120] This remark is translated in *Notes and Fragments* (2005:19).

[121] Kant had an edition of Seneca's philosophical works in his (relatively small) personal library (Warda 1922:55); Mendelssohn cites Seneca passim in his *Philosophical Writings* (but not the *Letters* themselves).

night sky figures prominently in Mendelssohn's rejoinder to the Burkean theorist who challenges him to show how the sublime can be accommodated within the perfectionist aesthetics of the German rationalist tradition: if natural sublimity is a matter of disorienting vastness and terrifying power, why be pleased by it?[122] In making his reply, Mendelssohn wants to hold on to the bivalence of our appreciation of sublimity: the sentiment involved has to be 'mixed' – it must gratify and overwhelm us at the same time, leaving us 'dizzy' and in some way unsettled. He begins with a relatively familiar list that spans both magnitudes of nature and spirit: '[t]he great world of the sea, a far-reaching plain, the innumerable legions of stars, the eternity of time, every height and depth that exhausts us, a great genius, great virtues that we admire but cannot attain: who can look upon these things without trembling?' (1997:144 [1929:I.398]). To respond to the Burkean theorist, he edits the list, removing undifferentiated, monotonous magnitudes, since with these 'discontent gains the upper hand': they are tedious, and even repulsive, because they offer no positive direction to thought. That leaves him with the starry night sky paired with greatnesses of spirit:

> By contrast, the immeasurable structure of the cosmos [*Unermeßlichkeit des Weltgebäudes*], the magnitude of an admirable genius or of sublime virtues are as differentiated as they are enormous, as perfect as they are differentiated, and the discontent bound up with the contemplation of them is grounded in our own weakness. Thus they afford an inexpressible pleasure of which the soul can never get enough.
>
> (1997:145 [1929:I.398]; translation altered)

Mendelssohn presents these remaining items on his list as differentiated, or articulated: the cosmos figures not as a random scatter of stars, but as the product of rational, and divine, creation. Our

---

[122] E.g., through the character Euphranor in the Eighth of the 'Letters on Sentiments' (1997:36 [1929:I.267–8]). On Mendelssohn's evolving response to Burke, see Koller (2011).

discontent in regarding the starry heavens, or considering the magnitude of genius or virtue, is a measure of our inchoate recognition of their greatness as rationally ordered perfections, paired with an awareness of our own 'weakness', or inability ever to replace that inchoate recognition with anything approaching full comprehension. Hence Mendelssohn's striking conclusion: although the discontent is grounded in our weakness, we remain *compelled* presumably because we recognise that the exalted rationality of the object, its ordered perfection, is a standard or law for us. 'No sense of tedium or revulsion, no discontent with this or that side of the object intermingles with our sentiment here, and we would be happy if our entire life could be an uninterrupted attempt to grasp the divine perfection' (1997:145 [1929:I.398–9]).[123] Does Mendelssohn manage, with this, to retain the bivalence proper to judgements of the sublime? The negative side of the experience is absorbed into the whole, as a tempered humility over our inability to comprehend fully the perfection that we are drawn to peer at, and admire.

Kant is closer to Mendelssohn in his famous 'starry heavens' passage that concludes the *Critique of Practical Reason* than he ever is in the Analytic of the Sublime two years later. In the famous passage, the starry heavens figure as an immeasurably structured system – not as a sheer vastness, or a disordered spray of stars.[124] But the passage also underscores aspects of Kant's account of the sublime that partly draw from Mendelssohn's insights and remain fully accommodated within the Analytic of the Sublime as well:

---

[123] See also the Third Letter (Theocles) earlier in the *Philosophical Writings*: 'The contemplation of the structure of the cosmos thus remains an inexhaustible source of pleasure for the philosopher. It sweetens his lonely hours, it fills his soul with the sublimest sentiments, withdrawing his thoughts from the dust of the earth and bringing them nearer to the throne of divinity' (1997:15 [1929:I.244]).

[124] Cf. CJ (5:270): 'if someone calls the sight of the starry heavens **sublime**, he must not ground such a judging of it on concepts of worlds inhabited by rational beings ... but must take it, as we see it, merely as a broad, all-embracing vault' – since an *aesthetic* judgement of reflection cannot determine the object under any concept.

above all, the idea that our enjoyment of natural sublime must involve a positive satisfaction of our rational capacity. For this is the basis on which Kant, like Mendelssohn before him, explains true sublimity not as a thrill that ultimately exhausts us, but as an enjoyment that draws from the satisfaction of reason and thereby stands to gather strength the more that it is sustained. However, whereas Mendelssohn takes this satisfaction to consist in some indistinct grasp of a rational order that is given to behold, and to be driven by admiration of the perfection of divine agency, Kant takes this satisfaction to lie in the arousal of *practical* reason, and to be driven by a commitment to *one's own* agency.

> Two things fill the mind with ever new and increasing admiration [*Bewunderung*] and reverence [*Ehrfurcht*] the more often and more steadily one considers them: *the starry heavens above me and the moral law within me* ... The first begins from the place I occupy in the external world of sense and extends the connection in which I stand into an unbounded magnitude with worlds upon worlds and systems of systems,[125] and moreover into the unbounded times of their periodic motion, their beginning and their duration. The second begins from my invisible self, my personality, and presents me in a world which has true infinity but which can be discovered only by the understanding.   (CPrR 5:161–2)

The starry night sky and the moral law within are not simply juxtaposed to one another, as models for looking up to something on high, or exalted, that share a basic shape. Rather, the recognition of one's real insignificance as an animal being in the order of cosmos *moves one* to the expression of a certain moral confidence, through a commitment to one's supersensible personality:

> The first view of a countless multitude of worlds annihilates, as it were, my importance as an *animal creature*, which after it has been for a short time provided with vital force (one knows not how) must

---

[125] Kant's language here is reminiscent of Alexander Pope, from the 1733 *Essay on Man*: 'See worlds on worlds compose one universe, Observe how system into system runs' (Pope 2016:8).

give back to the planet (a mere speck in the universe) the matter from which it came. The second, on the contrary, infinitely raises my worth as an *intelligence* by my personality, in which the moral law reveals to me a life independent of animality and even of the whole sensible world, at least so far as this may be inferred from the purposive determination [*Bestimmung*] of my existence by his law.

(5:162)

Thus, for Kant a person's enjoyment of the sublime turns upon her governing self-conception. Although considering my nothingness in relation to the vastness of the cosmos is unsettling, there must be something in me that remains untroubled by it, that accepts this calmly, if I am to enjoy a feeling of the sublime. The enjoyment requires a background commitment to make myself fit for my own essential rationality, i.e. to 'the purposive determination of my existence' as a *person* through the moral law.[126]

For Mendelssohn, the immeasurable perfection of divine creation, made manifest in the starry night sky, is paradigmatically sublime. One *looks out* and *loses oneself*, admiring the great goodness of divine creation. There is no sense in which one is implicitly admiring oneself, or even the highest possibility of *human* agency as such. Thus, whatever Mendelssohn might say, his invocations of the sublimity of human genius and virtue can only be, by his own lights, derivatives of this first and more paradigmatic case. But Kant cannot follow Mendelssohn on this path. He is blocked both by the epistemic principles of his critical philosophy, and by its metaphysics of value. Since Kant takes it that the divine intellect is *incomprehensible* to us, nothing we might say about the *rational* order of divine creation can be anything but a reflection of our finite cognitive power. For Kant, Mendelssohn's approach flirts with enthusiasm of another, more pernicious, sort: *Schwärmerei*, the presumption to have insight into what lies outside of the bounds of possible experience. Kant follows his 'starry heavens' passage with the caveat that while sublime feeling may appropriately inspire inquiry, it should never replace it (CPrR 5:162).

---

[126] This is, once again, the 'sublime' human *Bestimmung* introduced in §3.4.

Mendelssohn's aesthetic rationalism appeals to our (putative) power to appreciate the perfection of the cosmic order 'indistinctly', through feeling alone; Kant retorts that this may incite us to seek to understand what is not *there* to be understood. So he ends with the caveat that our awestruck admiration for the starry firmament, 'the noblest spectacle that can ever be present to the human senses', may well end 'in astrology' – if we presume that this noble spectacle expresses an interest in human affairs, and means to send us messages; and that even our respect for virtue, 'the noblest property of human nature', may well end 'in enthusiasm [*Schwärmerei*]' – if we presume to mingle in things divine, or to think we receive impressions of the effects of divine grace on our souls (CPrR 5:162).[127]

It follows from Kant's dualism of nature and freedom that there is no value in the world independently of reason, and nature is indifferent to us. Of course, the sublimity of *ashes to ashes, dust to dust* rests on this thought – and Kant makes apt use of it in the 'starry heavens' passage. Recognising our vanishing nothingness, as animal beings, we are pushed to consider our place in *another order*, the supersensible domain of freedom, the kingdom of ends. But this is not a consolation for our loss; it is not a promise of happiness. It points us towards every difficulty of the rational animal.

By contrast, some of the most powerful therapeutic arguments of Stoicism take the form of a consolation: this may seem bad – illness, exile, poverty, torture – but it isn't really. It was some such consolation that Seneca offered his mother from his exile in Corsica, when he wrote about his entranced study of the order and movements of the stars at night ('so long as my eyes are not directed away from that spectacle, which they can never look on enough ... what difference does it make to me what ground I tread?').[128] This is meant to contrast the self-seeking and

---

[127] Reading the remark about moral *Schwärmerei* to refer back to CPrR (5:85–6 and 127n), and religious *Schwärmerei* to anticipate Rel (6:53).
[128] *Consolation to Helvia* 8.6 (2014:56).

calculating exercise of reason that is so common in human affairs – and particularly in the cut-throat political circles of Rome. The petty striving of normal human affairs involves taking things to be good that are not in fact good, and becoming mad with frustration in one's failure to attain these spurious goods. So he has turned away from those small-minded agitations of thought, and loses himself in rationality on another order: one that embraces all there is. And this is good, because the tranquillity it affords is the basis of true happiness. However, such consolations are not available within Kantian thought.

References

1 Primary Sources

Kant

References to the works of Kant, with the exception of the *Critique of Pure Reason*, follow volume and page of the German Academy edition: *Kants Gesammelte Schriften*, edited by the Königlich Preußischen Akademie der Wissenschaften, later the Deutschen Akademie der Wissenschaften zu Berlin (Walter de Gruyter [and predecessors], 1902-). Quotations are drawn, with occasional modifications, from the translations in the following volumes of the Cambridge Edition of the Works of Immanuel Kant:

(1992) *Lectures on Logic*. Ed. J. Michael Young.
(1996) *Practical Philosophy*. Ed. Mary J. Gregor.
(1996) *Religion and Rational Theology*. Ed. Allen W. Wood and George di Giovanni.
(2002) *Critique of the Power of Judgment*. Ed. Paul Guyer.
(2005) *Notes and Fragments*. Ed. Paul Guyer.
(2007) *Anthropology, History, and Education*. Ed. Günter Zöller and Robert B. Louden.

I have consulted the following translations as well:

(1987) *Critique of Judgment*. Trans. Werner S. Pluhar. Indianapolis: Hackett.
(2003 [1929]) *Critique of Pure Reason*. Trans. Norman Kemp Smith. Basingstoke, Hampshire: Palgrave Macmillan.

I use the following abbreviations for Kant's works:

Anth	Anthropology from a Pragmatic Point of View
CJ	Critique of the Power of Judgment
CPR	Critique of Pure Reason
CPrR	Critique of Practical Reason

FI	First Introduction to the Critique of the Power of Judgment
JL	Jäsche Logic
MFNS	Metaphysical Foundations of Natural Science
MM	Metaphysics of Morals
MM-DV	Metaphysics of Morals, Doctrine of Virtue
Refl	Reflexionen (Academy volumes 14–17)
Rel	Religion within the Boundaries of Reason Alone
WIE	'What is Enlightenment'

Others

Ashfield, A. & de Bolla, P., eds. (1996). *The Sublime: A Reader in British Eighteenth-century Aesthetic Theory*. Cambridge: Cambridge University Press.

Baumgarten, A. G. (2007 [1750]). *Aesthetica/Ästhetik*, Latin-German edition. Trans. Dagmar Mirbach. Hamburg: Felix Meiner.

Bond, D. F., ed. (1965). *The Spectator*. Oxford: Clarendon Press.

Burke, E. (1990 [1757]). *A Philosophical Enquiry into the Origin of our Ideas of the Sublime and Beautiful*. Ed. Adam Phillips. Oxford: Oxford University Press.

Carter, E. (1817). *Letters from Mrs. Elizabeth Carter to Mrs. Montagu, Between the Years 1755 and 1800, Chiefly upon Literary and Moral Subjects*. Ed. Rev. Montagu Pennington. Volume 1. London: F. C. and J. Rivington.

Dennis, J. (1693). *Miscellanies in Verse and Prose*. London: James Knapton.

Gerard, A. (1759). *Essay on Taste: with Three Dissertations on the Same Subject by Mr. De Voltaire, Mr. D'Alembert, and Mr. De Montesquieu*. London and Edinburgh: A. Millar, A. Kincaid, and J. Bell.

Herder, J. G. (1998). Werke. Volume 8, *Schriften zu Literatur und Philosophie 1792–1800*. Frankfurt: Deutscher Klassiker Verlag.

Kames (Henry Home) (2005 [1785]). *Elements of Criticism*, sixth edition. Ed. Peter Jones, 2 vols. Indianapolis: Liberty Fund.

Long, A. A. & Sedley, D. N. (1987). *The Hellenistic Philosophers, 2 volumes*. Cambridge: Cambridge University Press.

Longinus (1995). *On the Sublime [ΠΕΡΙ ΥΨΟΥΣ]*. Trans. W. H. Fyfe, revised by Donald Russell. Cambridge: Harvard University Press.

Meier, G. F. (1757). *Betrachtungen über den ersten Grundsatz aller schönen Künste und Wissenschaften*. Halle: Carl Hermann Hemmerde.

Mendelssohn, M. (1929–). *Gesammelte Schriften: Jubiläumsausgabe.* Stuttgart/Bad Cannstatt: Frommann/Holzboog.

Mendelssohn, M. (1997 [1761]). *Philosophical Writings.* Trans. Daniel O. Dahlstrom. Cambridge: Cambridge University Press.

Pope, A. (2016). *An Essay on Man.* Ed. Tom Jones. Princeton: Princeton University Press.

Reid, T. (1969 [1785]). *Essays on the Intellectual Powers of Man.* Cambridge, MA: MIT Press.

Seneca, L. A. (1917 and 1925). *Epistles.* 2 vols. Trans. Richard M. Gummere. Cambridge, MA: Harvard University Press.

Seneca, L. A. (1928, 1932, and 1935). *Moral Essays.* 3 vols. Trans. John W. Basore. Cambridge, MA: Harvard University Press.

Seneca, L. A. (2010). *Anger, Mercy, Revenge.* Trans. Robert A. Kaster and Martha C. Nussbaum. Chicago: University of Chicago Press.

Seneca, L. A. (2014). *Hardship and Happiness.* Trans. Elaine Fantham, Harry M. Hine, James Ker, and Gareth D. Williams. Chicago: University of Chicago Press.

Seneca, L. A. (2015). *Letters on Ethics to Lucilius.* Trans. Margaret Graver and A. A. Long. Chicago: University of Chicago Press.

2 Secondary sources

Allison, H. (2001). *Kant's Theory of Taste.* Cambridge: Cambridge University Press.

Beiser, F. C. (2009). *Diotima's Children: German Aesthetic Rationalism from Leibniz to Lessing.* New York: Oxford University Press.

Brady, E. (2013). *The Sublime in Modern Philosophy: Aesthetics, Ethics, and Nature.* Cambridge: Cambridge University Press.

Brandt, R. (2003). The Vocation of the Human Being. In B. Jacobs and P. Kain, eds., *Essays on Kant's Anthropology.* Cambridge: Cambridge University Press, pp. 85–104.

Brennan, T. (2003). Stoic Moral Psychology. In B. Inwood, ed., *Cambridge Companion to the Stoics.* Cambridge: Cambridge University Press, pp. 257–94.

Budick, S. (2010). *Kant and Milton.* Cambridge, MA: Harvard University Press.

Budd, M. (2002). *The Aesthetic Appreciation of Nature.* Oxford: Clarendon Press.

Budd, M. (2008). *Aesthetic Essays.* Oxford: Oxford University Press.

Clewis, R. (2009). *The Kantian Sublime and the Revelation of Freedom.* Cambridge: Cambridge University Press.

Cochrane, T. (2012). The Emotional Experience of the Sublime. *Canadian Journal of Philosophy,* 42 (2), 125–48.

Crowther, P. (1989). *The Kantian Sublime.* Oxford: Clarendon Press.

Darwall, S. (1977). Two Kinds of Respect. *Ethics* 88 (1), 36–49.

Darwall, S. (2008). Kant on Respect, Dignity, and the Duty of Respect. In M. Betzler, ed., *Kant's Ethics of Virtue.* Berlin: de Gruyter, pp. 175–200.

di Giovanni, G. (2011). The Year 1786 and *Die Bestimmung des Menschen.* In R. Munk, ed., *Moses Mendelssohn's Metaphysics and Aesthetics.* Dordrecht: Springer, pp. 217–34.

Doran, R. (2015). *The Theory of the Sublime from Longinus to Kant.* Cambridge: Cambridge University Press.

Forsey, J. (2007). Is a Theory of the Sublime Possible? *Journal of Aesthetics and Art Criticism* 85 (4), 381–9.

Graver, M. (2016). Anatomies of Joy: Seneca and the *Gaudium* Tradition. In R. R. Caston and R. A. Kaster, eds., *Hope, Joy, and Affection in the Classical World.* Oxford: Oxford University Press, pp. 123–42.

Guyer, P. (1993). *Kant and the Experience of Freedom: Essays on Aesthetics and Morality.* Cambridge: Cambridge University Press.

Guyer, P. (2005). The Symbols of Freedom in Kant's Aesthetics. In *Values of Beauty: Historical Essays in Aesthetics.* Cambridge: Cambridge University Press, pp. 222–41.

Guyer, P. (2014). *A History of Modern Aesthetics.* Volume 1: The Eighteenth Century. Cambridge: Cambridge University Press.

Kennett, J. (2015). What is Required for Motivation by Principle? In G. Björnsson, C. Strandberg, R. F. Olinder, J. Eriksson, F. B. Björklund, eds., *Motivational Internalism.* New York: Oxford University Press, pp. 108–29.

Koller, A. (2011). Mendelssohn's Response to Burke on the Sublime. In R. Munk, ed., *Moses Mendelssohn's Metaphysics and Aesthetics.* Dordrecht: Springer, pp. 329–50.

Kuehn, M. (2009). Reason as a Species Characteristic. In A. Rorty and J. Schmidt, eds., *Kant's Idea for a Universal History with a Cosmopolitan Aim: A Critical Guide.* Cambridge: Cambridge University Press, pp. 68–93.

Lewis, C. T. & Short, C. (1879). *A Latin Dictionary.* Oxford: Clarendon Press.

Lyotard, J.-F. (1994). *Lessons on the Analytic of the Sublime*. Trans. E. Rottenberg. Stanford: Stanford University Press.

McDowell, J. (1979). Virtue and Reason. *The Monist* 62 (3), 331–50.

Merritt, M. (2011). Kant on Enlightened Moral Pedagogy. *Southern Journal of Philosophy* 49 (3), 227–53.

Merritt, M. (2012). The Moral Source of the Kantian Sublime. In T. Costelloe, ed., *The Sublime: from Antiquity to the Present*. Cambridge: Cambridge University Press, pp. 37–49.

Merritt, M. (2017). Sublimity and Joy: Kant on the Aesthetic Constitution of Virtue. In M. Altman, ed., *Palgrave Kant Handbook*. London: Palgrave Macmillan, pp. 447–67.

Merritt, M. (2018). *Kant on Reflection and Virtue*. Cambridge: Cambridge University Press.

Monk, S. H. (1960). *The Sublime*. Ann Arbor: University of Michigan Press.

Murdoch, I. (1999 [1959]). The Sublime and the Beautiful Revisited. In P. Conradi, ed., *Existentialists and Mystics: Writings on Philosophy and Literature*. New York: Penguin.

Rayman, J. (2012). *Kant on Sublimity and Morality*. Cardiff: University of Wales Press.

Reath, A. (1989). Kant's Theory of Moral Sensibility. *Kant Studien* 80 (1–4), 284–302.

Santozki, U. (2012). *Die Bedeutung antiker Theorien für die Genese und Systematik von Kants Philosophie*. Berlin: de Gruyter.

Schaper, E. (1992). Taste, Sublimity, and Genius: The Aesthetics of Nature and Art. In P. Guyer, ed., The Cambridge Companion to Kant. Cambridge: Cambridge University Press, pp. 367–93.

Sherman, N. (1997). *Making a Necessity of Virtue: Aristotle and Kant on Virtue*. Cambridge: Cambridge University Press.

Vogt, K. M. (2008). *Law, Reason, and the Cosmic City: Political Philosophy in the Early Stoa*. New York: Oxford University Press.

Warda, A. (1922). *Immanuel Kants Bücher*. Berlin: Martin Breslauer.

Zuckert, R. (2003). Awe or Envy: Herder contra Kant on the Sublime. *Journal of Aesthetics and Art Criticism* 61 (3), 217–32.

Printed in the United States
By Bookmasters